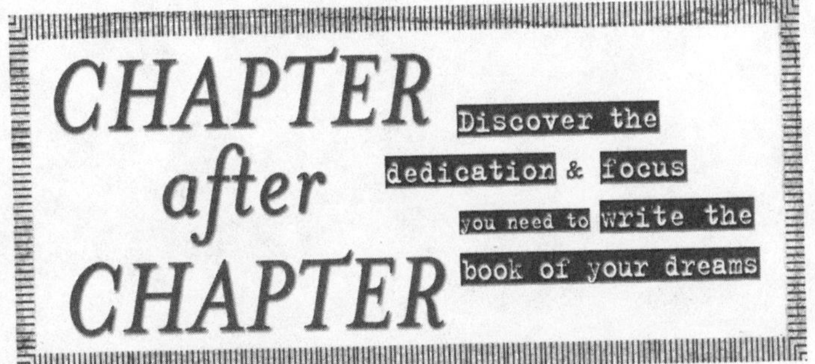
CHAPTER
after
CHAPTER
Discover the
dedication & focus
you need to write the
book of your dreams

CHAPTER *after* CHAPTER

Discover the dedication & focus you need to write the book of your dreams

WRITER'S DIGEST BOOKS
CINCINNATI, OHIO
www.writersdigest.com

HEATHER SELLERS
author of Page After Page

 Published by Writer's Digest Books, an imprint of F+W Publications, Inc., 4700 East Galbraith Road, Cincinnati, OH 45236. (800) 289-0963. First edition.

Distributed in Canada by Fraser Direct, 100 Armstrong Avenue, Georgetown, ON, Canada L7G 5S4, Tel: (905) 877-4411. Distributed in the U.K. and Europe by David & Charles, Brunel House, Newton Abbot, Devon, TQ12 4PU, England, Tel: (+44) 1626 323200, Fax: (+44) 1626 323319, E-mail: postmaster@davidandcharles.co.uk. Distributed in Australia by Capricorn Link, P.O. Box 704, Windsor, NSW 2756 Australia, Tel: (02) 4577-3555.

Visit our Web site at www.writersdigest.com for information on more resources for writers.

To receive a free weekly e-mail newsletter delivering tips and updates about writing and about Writer's Digest products, register directly at our Web site at http://newsletters.fwpublications.com.

11 10 09 08 07 5 4 3 2 1

Library of Congress Cataloging-in-Publication Data

Sellers, Heather
Chapter after chapter: discover the dedication & focus you need to write the book of your dreams / Heather Sellers. -- 1st ed.
p. cm.
ISBN-13: 978-1-58297-425-5 (hardcover : alk. paper)
ISBN-10: 1-58297-425-X (hardcover : alk. paper)
1. Authorship. I. Title.
PN147.S37 2007
808'.02--dc22 2006024636

Edited by Kelly Nickell
Designed by Lisa Kuhn and Claudean Wheeler
Illustrations by Paine Proffitt
Production coordinated by Mark Griffin
Heather Sellers photograph © Face Photography

Also by Heather Sellers

Page After Page: Discover the Confidence & Passion You Need to Start Writing & Keep Writing

Spike and Cubby's Ice Cream Island Adventure

Drinking Girls and Their Dresses

Georgia Under Water

Your Whole Life

Dedication

For my brilliant editor, Kelly Nickell, co-author, teacher, and dear friend, most patient, wise, instructive, kind. So much of this book is yours, all the way through, including the original idea. I am so grateful to you for every single page of this project.

About the Author

Heather Sellers is a professor of English at Hope College in Holland, Michigan, where she teaches creative writing and writes every day. She has just completed a memoir, *Face First*, and a new textbook for the college classroom, *The Practice of Creative Writing*. Her fiction and poetry appear regularly in journals and anthologies. She enjoys public speaking, triathlons, cooking, kids, and growing Japanese vegetables. Her Web site is www.heathersellers.com.

Acknowledgments

My students—to whom this book is written—I am so grateful to you all. Special support was provided by Kristin Olson, Bethany Katerberg, Chantelle Kramer, Keri Maxon, Meghan Florian, Jordan Wolfson, Lauren Eriks, Ashley Perez, Matthew Baker, Christian Piers, Laura Woltag, Emily Burns, Michele Lindstedt, Nicole Brace, Marilyn Churchill, Bruce Berg, and Elena Valle. I owe much to Lorraine Lopez, whose wisdom saves me again and again. Gratitude to Kelly Nickell, Greg Hatfield, Linda Walker, Jane Friedman, Barbara Kuroff, and the staff at Writer's Digest for their kindness and hard work. I deeply appreciate the support of Hope College, its English department, the library, the Department of Sociology and Social Work, and Lisa Lampen. Thanks to Till Midnight for the high top by the windows and to Heather Dibkey for the flowers and the muscles. Thanks to Tom Valeo for reminding me of a necessary book (*Writing for Story*) at the exact right moment and to Patricia Sarrafian Ward for Chapter One. To Lynn Japinga (thanks for walking) and Annie Japinga (thanks for walking the dog). David DeZwaan, as always. Elaura Niles, Janis Arnold, Alyssa Leal, Amy Fusselman, Debra Wierenga, Betsey Kepes, Dinty Moore, Anne Turkle, Pat Roehling, Lorna Hernandez Jarvis, Estella Blevins, Rosemary Cantor—thank you for everything you have shared with me along the way. I am always learning and borrowing from these teachers and their work: Gingah Knuth, Janet Burroway, Jack Ridl. William Kooistra, Jr., thank you for life-changing conversations.

Table of Contents

Introduction .... *page* [1]

PART 1
Your Writing Wings: Surveying the Book-Writing Terrain

Chapter 1: Rose to Ash .... *page* [8]
Clinging to writing ideas squeezes the life out of them. Loosen your grip. Saving a book idea is deadly.

Chapter 2: Limits .... *page* [13]
Why *not* having unlimited time and unlimited funding helps your book get written right on schedule.

Chapter 3: Books Plural, and Under the Bed .... *page* [21]
A writing life is a long-term commitment. Think in terms of writing a series of books. Starting the first one will suddenly become possible.

Chapter 4: The Book 100 .... *page* [28]
Adapted from the Pilates strength-training program used by professional football players and dancers, this exercise helps you to build a strong foundation for writing effective books.

Chapter 12: Layers of Should .... *page* [87]
When you get stuck on a book project, there is almost always more than one reason you aren't making forward progress. Examine your relationship to what you think you should do and clear the way for the book you want to write.

Chapter 13: Good Enough.................................. *page* [98]
How perfect does your book have to be? How do you know what still needs work? When is it Good Enough?

Chapter 14: Faith in Writing ....*page* [104]
Believing in your book—that it's good, that it means something, that it even exists—takes a special kind of commitment. Call it faith.

Chapter 15: You're Ready Now.........................*page* [109]
In order to learn how to write a book, you must write a book. In fact, your book-in-progress turns out to be the perfect writing teacher for you. You are absolutely ready.

PART 2
The Long Haul: Strength-Building for Book Writers

Chapter 16: Wise Guides...............................*page* [116]
Writing a book is a bit like going off alone to a desert island. You get to take some books with you on your journey; will you pack wisely, with intention?

Chapter 24: Stuck/Unstuck .... *page* [166]
Writing a book is a process of getting stuck and unstuck. Techniques to free yourself from common writing quagmires.

PART 3
Your Written Words Take Shape: Declaring Your Book Finished

Chapter 25: Writing Is Revising .... *page* [176]
Revision isn't a do-over. It's re-seeing what you have written. Experienced writers use re-seeing as the mainstay of a writing practice.

Chapter 26: Just Want to Be Done .... *page* [182]
There is pressure to finish too quickly and submit your book before it is ready. How to manage the fiercely proud "I'm Done" devil.

Chapter 27: Reality Agents .... *page* [187]
Searching for the right agent can be as consuming and difficult as writing a book. A closer look at agents and their role in the publishing process reminds you that you have many options and a lot of power as an author.

Chapter 28: Not Too Old, Not Too Late .... *page* [197]
Two popular yet very unconvincing excuses for not finishing your book: "I'm too old" and "It's too late." Also: "I'm too young" and "It's too soon." Dopey reasons for quitting/not starting exposed for what they really are.

Introduction

LEARNING TO WRITE BOOKS IS JUST AS HARD AS LEARNING TO write, period. A lot of people think because they know how to write, they'll just write a book. But creating a book-length work is a whole thing unto itself, with quirks and lessons and challenges not found in any other endeavor. This book hopes to light the path, at least a little, so you can see what's up ahead and prepare accordingly.

There are many fine books on how to write a novel, a memoir, a children's book. Also, there are useful books on how to publish, how to find an agent, how to locate a writing conference. You can find a book on how to write dialogue, opening paragraphs, sonnets, the first five pages, the truth, fantasy novels, romance stories, with style, on weekends, starting with endings.

This book is different. It's partly a meditation on the art of writing—in this case, the art of writing a book. And it's partly an approach to a special kind of writing life. It's partly memoir and partly inspiration to motivate you as you write your own book. Each chapter in *Chapter After Chapter* comes with an exercise (or two) designed to help you finish your book—the book you are meant to write.

These exercises might seem easy, delicious, distracting, annoying, peculiar, or all of those things at once. I use them in my own writing groups and in my advanced classes; they sometimes help my students to break through a small psychological block. Or, at least chip away at the cement a little. I urge you to do the exercises on paper and not in your head like everyone is tempted to do. Do the ones that seem least helpful; often it is in the places we *don't notice anything interesting* that there is room for the most growth.

A failing we writers have is that we confuse the voices in our heads with writing; we tend to do exercises in our heads because *thinking* and *writing* feel so closely related. Visual artists never have this problem. Their sketchbooks are filled with sketches; when they do an exercise, they can't just do it in their minds.

Writing is a physical art. And writing a book is a lot more like making a complex sculpture out of bronze than like writing a bunch of reports. What's in your head does not count, not for sculpture, not for book writing. Pencil on paper is what matters. Words on paper, pages and pages, chapter after chapter.

Visual artists don't ask people to look at their *ideas* for paintings—they go ahead and paint pictures. Book authors don't trade in ideas, either. Ideas are worthless; everyone has them. In order to start your book project, you have to give up the idea habit. No more ideas.

So, doing the exercises is vital. You have to *write* to write a book. To keep you honest and focused, you may want to do the exercises in a group. By creating a small group engaged in a common task and working together with shared deadlines, you'll find your writing powers growing by leaps and bounds; most people are amazed. Especially those who hate exercise-y things (like me).

I learn best when someone tells me a story. I'm like my friend Lucinda, who goes to a faculty meeting and cannot for the life of her comprehend what is going on and who afterwards has to ask a colleague, "What was that about?" By which she means, "What story just took place in that room?"

So here are the stories I've learned about writing books, the stories I have been told, the stories that have helped me stay the course or get back on it when I have lost my hope, lost my way, lost my mind, lost my voice, lost my place.

There's a myth that once you reach book publication, you can sit back and drink champagne and books pop out of you like hen eggs and Oprah calls you and you look younger and younger each year ...

No.

It's so hard.

When people say, "I have an idea for a book!" to those of us working on our books, we cringe a little. When you have an idea, you have nothing particularly special—yet. A lot of people have ideas for books. The real question is: What are you going to do with it?

You already love to write. You work at it, play with it, wonder a lot about how the world of books and authors works, what it all means, and how to participate meaningfully. Writing is how you know who you are. If you're reading this book, perhaps you want to see not only your book more clearly, but yourself, too. Writing is still the best tool I have found for understanding almost anything at all.

We need more books. We need *your* book. The world is improved significantly when more people know other people's points of view. What could be more democratic, more peace oriented, more problem solving than a world where each person's vision, each person's statement on some tiny slice of life is present, accounted for, bound, and available? Books do not have to be great. They can be good enough. We simply need to move toward *the complete set.* By writing your book, are you doing the world a favor? Maybe, possibly, you really are. It's a fact that keeping your book as an idea is not helping anyone. Possibly, it's hurting you.

I fear a lot of people—my parents, my friends, my students, myself—stay stuck in *wanting.* We're on the verge of creative power, of hooking into a new energy source—a truly up-and-running book project is a great source of energy!—but we linger, frozen kids on the high dive. Fear closes in, strangles us from making a move. We close tightly around the old self, the never-jumped-off-the-diving-board self. And we're all poorer for it.

Being on the verge is usually the scariest part. Scarier than climbing up the ladder. Much, much scarier than when you walked-didn't-run to get in line for this great new experience—*I am going to write a book!*

The scariest part is just before you jump.

I'd like to give you the gentlest push. I'd like to nudge you toward the deep end. I'd like to hold your hand on the way down, and grin at you underwater, and make sure you are pointed to the swim ladder, and laugh with you when you come up for air, and say in unison with you, "Let's do it again!"

Writing a book is like plunging off the high dive. It's scary and thrilling and weird—you aren't in the shallow end anymore, hanging with the little kids. And you can never really go back there and fit in again. And there may be sharks in the deep end, even if only in your mind: jealous friends and cranky bosses and stressed-out family members and tortured people who can't be happy for you even if you are living your dream. But that's what this book is for.

This book tries to shine light on the *inside* and on the blank pages before you. I hope to give you some shark management tools and some lures to help you attract your own personal muse. Even if you aren't sure you're ready to write a book, doing the exercises and reading these stories will—I hope!—help you to clarify your ideas, enrich your writing practice, and feel more confident about what it is you have to say and the right you have to say it.

Part 1

Your Writing Wings: Surveying the Book-Writing Terrain

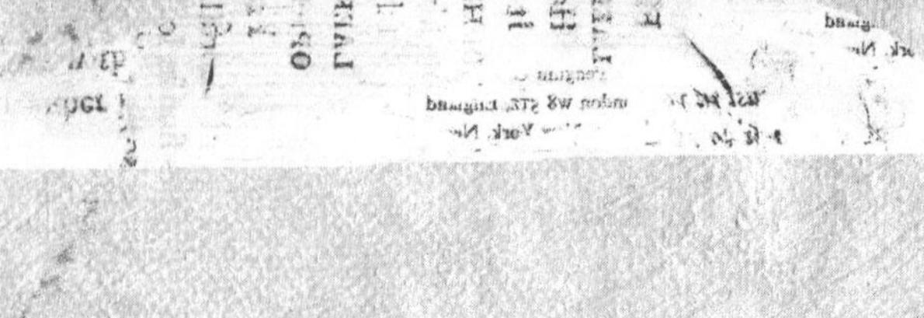

Chapter 1

Rose to Ash

IMAGINE YOU WANT A PERFECT ROSE MORE THAN ANYTHING in the world.

You get your rose.

There will never be another rose this perfect.

You want to keep this fresh perfect rose forever. It's almost too perfect to look at now. You want to save it so you can look at it later, always.

You don't want to do anything to lose this rose.

So you put it in a safe. Lock it up.

A year later, you decide it's time to look at your perfect rose.

You open the safe.

You look inside.

Ash.

The rose has turned to ash.

You are devastated. You didn't spend much time looking at it when it was fresh because you were saving it, saving it for now. And it's gone.

Ideas in writing work the same way.

One writer I know, Brandon, is dying to write what he calls his magnum opus, a fantasy novel that brings all of his ideas together in one stunning story. But he feels stuck as a writer, completely blocked, and he has trouble starting even small pieces. Many of his friends have told him he needs to write his magnificent book and risk failure in order to save it. The longer he sits on his project, the more blocked Brandon will become.

But he won't start writing.

Brandon works at a flower shop during the day. He lives with his parents—he has the time and the money to write. He says he wants to hone his technique on smaller pieces, shorter fantasy stories. He keeps a journal. He jots down his ideas. He *thinks* about his book.

No good.

When most writers try to write down their *ideas* for stories, they usually only capture a tiny bit of the work from a faraway, not creative place in their minds. They keep the story itself locked away in a safe. Fresh and perfect. *Idea*lized for all eternity.

Do not save up ideas. Do not write about the work from a distance. Instead of writing notes about an idea like *story about babysitter*, write: *Dana said, "You didn't pay me last time, either, Heather." And she smacked that gum which seemed to be a weird striped gum, green and purple, both.*

Write down what you hear. Write down what you see. These are the tiny squares of fabric that become the quilt that is the piece.

Transition out of ideas and into *images*.

You will be amazed at the results you get when you start doing this, working like a real writer.

Writers work in terms of images. That means: writing it down, working it up. You can't put images and story ideas and creative notions away for later. They will not be there. Don't keep your *horse novel idea* in the safe. When you sit down to write your novel's first sentence, nothing will come.

Nothing will be there.

The idea will have turned to ash.

Never again say, "I have an idea for a book." Don't be like the man I met in a hotel hot tub in Florida when I was speaking at a writing conference. He said, "I have ideas for five books. Do you know what software I should get?"

He was not a writer attending the conference. He was with his girlfriend. He had her. And a real estate license. And he had ideas.

"Software?" I said.

"Yeah. You know. The software makes out the structure and you fill it in. They have programs. Do you know a good one?"

You're the program, baby, I did not say.

It's comfortable, satisfying, and fear reducing, like a baby pacifier, to have ideas for books. Book ideas are reassuring and interesting, like imaginary friends.

The idea stage. It's a stage that writers who want to sustain writing lives must pass through very quickly, very firmly, with confidence. Many writers get stuck in ideas, sucked in.

Not you.

It's time to cultivate real relationships with other working writers and with your own working manuscript.

The best way to purge yourself of the comforting fantasy of the idea stage is to do one very important thing: Write.

Got an idea?

WRITE.

Don't think. Don't harbor. Don't daydream.

Just write it down.

That's the difference between writers and wannabes,

between writers and regular citizens. Writers make the effort, they take the plunge.

Writers write things down.

There's a productive alchemy with words on paper: Ideas in head = rose to ash. Words on paper = book germinating, piece developing.

Words on paper are real.

Reverse your field. If you spend 90 percent of your creative energy dreaming of a book and dreaming of the writing life, and only 10 percent of your time actually writing, you need to flip it around.

Give 90 percent of your energy to the words on the page.

Writing a book is accomplished by writing, chapter after chapter after chapter.

ON YOUR PAGE: *Exercise 1*

Pretend you've just been abducted by aliens. They will return you to Earth and your family (if you want to be returned), but first they insist you write a book. They're giving you ten minutes, and if you do not comply, they will blow up the planet. All of mankind depends on you writing the book. Set your timer.

Don't write *about* the book.

Write the book.

Type fast. Write the part that comes to you first—it doesn't matter if it is not the beginning.

If it is your horse novel, just do the part where the horse is leaping with the poor tuberculosis girl, over the stream, racing through the woods. Just write that part.

Go! Go! Go!

Now.

Whew! You got a piece of your book out of your head where you were killing it and into the light where it may have a chance to survive.

Repeat.

Hit on another part of the same book, or do a whole new one.

Ten minutes.

In this way, you make a bouquet of (imperfect) roses. You no longer put a rose in a safe. You know what to do with these fresh flowers: Give them water. Feed them.

Pick one.

Write your book every day.

Chapter 2
Limits

THE NUMBER ONE REASON BOOKS DON'T GET FINISHED IS this: *Writers say yes to other things.*

Successful book writers are very rarely also: historical society presidents, garden club secretaries, book group members, room mothers, rumba instructors, feng shui consultants, yoga expert students, and leaders of the town's spring clean-up committee. When you're writing a book, you do not have time for: meetings, grant writing, sonnet competitions, sprawling vacations, breeding dogs, renovating a bathroom, honing your poker skills for the circuit, or starting a nonprofit. When you're actively writing a book, you're in one giant glorious Time-Out From Hobbies.

Most of the book authors I know limit themselves to one "extracurricular." The key difference between successful book writers and failed, not-finishing book writers is this: When they're struggling with the book, the successful writers let the extracurriculars go, not the book-writing effort.

It's easy for us to instruct our children on how to cut back on extra activities and television and instant messaging in order to focus on a difficult school project, but we can't apply the same clear principle to our own book writing. We can help other people set limits, but what about when it comes to our own work? Why is it so hard for book writers to realize the book takes up a lot of space in life?

In order to write a book, you can't do a lot of other stuff. Things have to be put on hold until you are finished with the book. After you're done with your novel, you can do that eight-week turn on your church finance committee, and you can rejoin the gospel choir. But when you are actively writing, you are married to the book. The rest of the stuff has to wait.

When Betsey decided to write her young adult novel, she started on January 1, just like her favorite author, Isabel Allende, always does. The first thing Betsey did was set up her weekly writing schedule in her planner—she penned in the hours using red ink, just like you would if you had a job that required you to make appointments with people all over town. Alongside her sons' play rehearsals and dentist appointments, there were hours that said *Leonora,* the working title of her novel.

If she missed book time because someone was sick or she overslept or company was in town, she made a note of it and paid herself back. The time came from *somewhere*, and it came out of the hide of life, not the hide of the book.

Betsey hooked all of her writing sessions to something else she was already doing. During the week, after she dropped her son off at school, she shot over to the library for two hours. After she taught piano lessons on Fridays and Saturdays, she wrote. In her planner, she wrote the title of her book, and she gave it an hour, just like it was another student. Which in a way, it really was.

A lot of ready-to-write-a-book authors jump in like fad dieters, making radical changes: *I will write every day this summer!* They don't make a realistic plan on how to fit writing into their daily lives. And after week three, they creep away (see Chapter 7: Surround Sound), and then by July, they aren't even thinking about the book anymore. They're in North Carolina with their in-laws, thinking about barbecued ribs, Uncle Tony's secret affair, and whether the kids should go to the movies or hang out with the family.

When you impose new rules, you have to give yourself fair warning. If you're going to write a novel this summer, get in shape this spring with little daily writing sessions. You need to pack for the trip. You can't just change the rules on a dime and expect success.

Start slow.

My yoga teacher says if it hurts your knees to sit on the floor in the classic meditation position, sit on a Chicago phone book until your body releases, becomes more flexible. Every day, you tear out one page of the phone book. And when the book is empty, you're on the floor in perfect position *and you won't even notice any pain.*

That's what you need to do to set up a book-writing life. Ease yourself into it so you're not asking yourself to do too much, give up too much all at once. Most people just aren't realistic about how much time it takes to write a book and what they'll have to sacrifice to do it right.

There are limits.

There are limits as to what you can do in your real life if you want to be a dedicated book writer.

If you're not good at making time to sit down and write every day, give yourself a month to learn how to do just that. Try to find fifteen minutes a day. Delete a television show or a meeting or quit doing the dishes after dinner. If you can't do fifteen minutes, start with five. Go sit in your writing room for five minutes a day for a month. Do exercises—perhaps like the ones in this book—or just let yourself daydream. Write by hand, slowly, making little notes and sketches. *Ease* yourself into a disciplined writing life.

It's like training for a race. You need to log miles of pages before you start writing the actual book. If you don't, if you dive right in without any advance warning, your real life will probably hijack your book. You'll lose ground. Months will pass, no book written, just a bunch of starts. I have done this so many times!

Start slowly. Set and reset your goals, little by little transforming your life into the life of a focused writer. Refuse to miss a day. Start adding a minute to each session. If you miss a day, pay yourself back, pronto.

Train first. Then climb Mt. Everest.

I know a man who wrote his detective novel on forty-minute lunch breaks. During his morning commute, he planned his writing session. Every lunch hour, he sat in his car in the parking lot and wrote. On weekends, he rewrote. He never talked about his project. He just *got it done*. He never missed a day of work. (Either kind of work.) His daily schedule, like Betsey's pupils, made for a nice set of limits around which he framed his writing time. That time was already part of his life. And since no one ever comes up to people in cars in parking lots, he created a bubble of bracketed time for himself and never, ever missed a day of writing.

To write a romance novel, you probably need a year of limits: You'll need your evenings and most weekends, too. My friend Rachel worked at a demanding ad agency from 8 A.M.

to 5 P.M., often getting home after 6 P.M. Instead of relaxing when she got home, she ate dinner at her writing desk and wrote from 7 to 11 P.M. four nights a week. Most weekends, she wrote for five hours a day. She skipped Thanksgiving dinner (her mother is *still* pissed at her), but she took two weeks off at Christmas, after which she embarked on a full revision of the whole manuscript. During the year of the book, Rachel's friends were cranky, but her husband was incredibly supportive. She didn't go to the gym, and she gained twenty-seven pounds (she looks beautiful, like a confident woman from a painting). She missed *Sex and the City, The Sopranos,* the Stones tour, and many, many fun things.

She also created an incredible dream world and had imaginary friends (the characters in her book) to keep her company every single night.

In May, she sent her manuscript to several agents. Four months later, she had a contract for a three-book deal!

She got a *ton* of money. After the sale, she took all her friends to dinner and her mother on a cruise. She quit her job, and she and her husband moved to Florida. Rachel's a full-time writer now.

Last year, *you* spent thirteen hundred hours *doing stuff.*

Rachel corralled her hours. She cut the fat out of her life. She ate at her desk. She worked hard. She wanted to become a full-time, well-paid writer, so she hired herself (without pay) and did what full-time, well-paid writers do: Write. A lot.

It was a gamble, with limits.

At a conference I attended this weekend, I learned that John Updike, the fantastic American novelist and writer, doesn't know who Madonna is. Madonna! John Updike doesn't read grocery store magazines, listen to regular radio, or watch television. He is removed. You may not want to go that far, but it's important to control the amount of Transitory World you take in. Successful writers limit what goes into their brains, what taxes their time, and they select for quality. Once you know how much time you can realistically devote to writing each week, you'll be able to free up your mind and give more attention to your family and your day job. And, ultimately, more to your book.

At a recent conference in Florida, I asked the attendees to make a list of the activities they couldn't possibly live without—the activities essential to their daily lives. Then I asked them to circle three activities they could eliminate during their book-writing time. Members of the audience read their final lists of Cannot Live Withouts, and the rest of us clapped for each item we thought was truly essential to the life of a soon-to-be-published writer.

"Book group," one woman read from her list. The crowd went wild. Everyone clapped.

I said, "Really?"

Most writers I know can't be in book groups while they themselves are actively writing a book—they just don't have the time to do both.

"Bunco," another woman read from her list. Half the room clapped.

Hmmm.

"Maybe I wasn't clear," I said louder. "We're only clapping if this is an essential activity. Something a writer can't live without during the book-writing year." I nodded in a teacher-like way and called on someone else.

"Choir!" she said. Everyone clapped enthusiastically.

I gave up.

If choir feeds your soul, which feeds your writing, then it is truly a fabulous way to get a book written.

This exercise was disastrous for me as a teacher, but I believe it's a reality for anyone wanting to get her book written. A lot of people say they want to write a book when really they like to be around books and writers and readers. Nothing wrong with that. It's just important to know, deeply and utterly, which kind of person you are. Can you set limits in order to birth a healthy book? Are you really going to do this thing?

In the words of my dramatic mother, "Are you willing to make the ultimate sacrifice?" By which she never meant death, just missing dessert.

ON YOUR PAGE: *Exercise 2*

Get ready to the clear the decks. Choose a start date when you will officially go into Book Author mode. Be realistic about how much time you have and how much time writing a book will take.

Literally do the math. How long will it take to write this book, based on the hours you honestly have? Do you have ten hours a week blocked in? Three? Twelve? This will change as you work, and that's fine. You need to figure out a basic plan and involve your loved ones in order to get support. (Remember Rachel's supportive husband?)

Imagine how long your chapters will be. How many will you need? Just make a rough estimate. Build in extra time for illness, being sidetracked, and computer disasters. Overestimate by 10 or 20 percent.

How many years will your book take? Seven years? Ten? That's okay. Don't despair. Did you write a book in the last eleven years? You will this time. Break it down into little pieces, like you would if you were telling a kid how to stay motivated on a long-term project. After laying out the big picture, focus on today. This week. This month. Use a calendar.

Next, set limits. Do you need to throw more activities overboard? You can live without television (many book authors just don't have time to watch). You can live without girls' night out. You can live without ________________________.

Be real. Make a list of what can be eliminated during the book-writing year. Remember, once the book is done, you can go hog-wild and overbook yourself like a little maniac. (But I bet you don't.)

Chapter 3

Books Plural, and Under the Bed

THE VERY FAMOUS VISITING WRITER WAS SCHEDULED TO arrive in seven minutes, and I was on my hands and knees, crawling along the edge of Hope College's fanciest conference room, the Maas Auditorium.

The Maas Auditorium, a dark-paneled intimidating place, is outfitted with high-tech screens and speakers, and I was scrambling to find a plug for the microphone and tape recorder. I had six minutes to activate the whole complicated system and get my introduction ready, and I couldn't find anything that looked like an outlet. I tapped and stroked the walls, toed the carpeting, flicked switches, and waited for the voice of God to boom, "Step away from the podium."

At last I dashed into the adjacent kitchen and among the refrigerators and floral arrangements and stainless steel sinks, I twirled around. "Help," I said. "Help. Anyone?"

Sharon (her name was in red cursive across her breast pocket), one of the conference coordinators, appeared from the deep aluminum recesses of the kitchen. "I can help," she said. She smiled.

"I'm sorry to be so last minute," I said. I grabbed her hand and pulled her into the Maas. "I'm desperate for an outlet. A plug," I said.

"Sure," she said, as though I was making sense. (People can be so nice.)

Sharon, holding one end of the cord that came out of my tape player, tapped the walls and looked under the tables and felt around the inside of the podium, just like I had done, and I walked around behind her with the microphone and cords feeling very much like I was her IV pole.

Suddenly she said, "You're Heather Sellers, aren't you? You wrote a children's book?"

We stopped short.

I looked at the clock.

"I wrote one children's book, *Spike and Cubby*." The writer was on his way. He'd be here in three minutes. Normally I would have been thrilled to talk about my book, about all children's books. Any other time I would have told her how Amy, the illustrator, did all the hard parts, and how much I learned from her. How it's not just the story of our two real-life dogs, her Spike and my Cubby—how it also teaches about the creative process (Cubby, like me, is a writer) and the way play and work dance together to enable concentration and focus.

Sharon dropped her end of the cord and said, passionately, "I want to write a children's book about Sinter Klaus. There isn't one. And it's such a great story."

"A wonderful story!" I said. I was starting to get really nervous.

"My kids and I have been doing research. There's so much history in the story, and I think people need to know about Sinter Klaus."

I said, "Can you come to my office and we can talk? I'd love to tell you what I know. Anytime? I'd be *happy to.*" I was tapping the mike in my palm, sweating. "Maybe an extension cord?" I said. "We can run into the kitchen? Or something?"

I envisioned the Very Famous Visiting Writer tripping, falling. Duct tape. I really wanted to write down "SCBWI" and "Nancy Lamb" and "Read 100" on scrap paper for kind Sharon. I didn't want to blow her off at all. "It's great you want to write," I said.

She smiled. "I just want to write *one book*. Before I die. I want to cross that off my list."

I kneeled down. I looked under the table. I said, to the floor, "I want to talk about this with you. But I am so nervous about the setup for the room right now."

Sharon said, "Here's a plug!"

And the writer walked in.

As Sharon walked out with my contact information, I kept thinking about her and her wish: *I just want to write one book*.

The tape player worked. The Very Famous Visiting Writer brilliantly took the students through a short story, and they asked good questions. He asked them each their names. And as he described how he'd published seven books, my thoughts returned to Sharon.

How many people have you heard say, "All I want to do is write *one* book"?

Some people want to be *writers*—they want to work on book after book for the love of the craft. Others just want to write one book—just to do it. And there's nothing wrong with that, but the idea perplexes me.

The process of learning to write a book is so intensive and consuming that I think it defies *single attempts*. Would someone go to Wimbledon to play *one match*? Become a heart surgeon just to do one open-heart surgery and then go back to his regular life? Would someone go to law school to try just *one* case in court? Or go through all the trouble of opening a coffee shop to stay open for one day? You might think I'm being melodramatic, but the point is that writing is hard; it can take a lifetime to learn the skills necessary to be successful.

You go to Wimbledon because you're a tennis player. Tennis is what you do. Wimbledon is just another part of the process. You become a lawyer to protect the rights of others. You open a coffee shop because you love coffee. And you write books because you're a writer, living the writing life.

Writers write *books.* Plural.

I believe (and you may disagree) that wanting to write just one book is not going to work for very many people. Maybe you know lots of people who are exceptions. For me, learning the craft of writing is simply too much of a time investment to write one book. It took me seven years to learn how to write a book and three years more to get one published.

If you are a writer, you are a writer. For life. It consumes a pretty big part of your identity. Writing books, like having kids, isn't really a *sideline.* It's not a list item. It's a way of living.

Some of the books you write are probably going to be awful. Especially the first ones. This is why you have to be willing to write more than one book. What works best is to say, "I have an idea. I will practice writing a book with this idea. It might not work. I will have more ideas, and I will write more books in order to learn what I need to know."

Have you read former Poet Laureate Billy Collins' first book of poetry? Or the earliest work of Eudora Welty? Michael Crichton's first draft of his first book? Not many people have. Why? Because they're not great books. Billy

Collins' first book of poetry isn't even in print anymore. The poems are fine. But they aren't great. They aren't like the poems he writes now. Billy Collins has gotten *better.* A lot better, with each book. Successful authors keep going. And going. And going. They're in for the long haul. Learning how to write takes too much energy, too much preparation, and too much of a commitment to do it for just one book.

You may be thinking, *But what about Harper Lee? She only wrote one book.*

Well, she only *published* one book. Who knows how many books she's actually written. Don't get me wrong. There's nothing wrong with writing one book, but most people find it necessary to write many books to write *one great book*.

This is why successful writers, those who go on to become published writers, write *books*, plural. Because some of these books *never see the light of day.*

Here's the Super Secret. The book writer's clubhouse password, what you have to be able to say to get in the room:

There are book manuscripts under my bed.

In order to write a truly great book, a publishable book, you write the training books, the "starter" books. Then, you bury the bodies. Can you skip the books-under-the-bed part? Can you learn to write books in another way?

Sure. But you're still likely to accumulate a few under-the-bed books at some point in your writing life, and that's okay. It's normal. All writers do this.

When novelist Janis Arnold started her first book, *Daughters of Memory*, it seemed to write itself.

After it was published, Janis started on her next book. But it was too terrible to even finish. Then, she started *another* book. Her editor said about that one: "This goes under the bed." He actually used those words. It's the clubhouse password. (Janis keeps the draft in the bottom drawer of an ancient filing cabinet in her study and not under her bed, which she fears would give her uneasy sleep and annoy her housekeeper, but it's close enough.) She started her next new book and knew right away her editor would hate it, so she cut out the middleman and put it "under the bed" with its dusty dear sister.

Then she wrote a keeper: *Excuse Me for Asking.* Janis went in an atypical order. Her under-the-bed books came after a first-book success. But the writing muses require regular sacrifices. They must be paid.

How-to-write books are good to use as resources, but the best way to learn how to write is to *write your book*. As many drafts as it takes. And then write your next book. You will learn more by practicing than you will in class. Writing classes and how-to books may save you time, but they won't replace practice.

Personally, I have four very beloved under-the-bed books. They're like former friends. They take up psychic energy, but not a lot of it. We had a relationship. I learned things. From the college novel, I learned that characters without perspective on the world or themselves are difficult to use as the center of a novel. From the single-mom novel, I learned that the "write-your-novel-in-thirty-days" and "plots-for-dummies" plans are *not* helpful; they produce dumb books even if the plots are fine. From writing my memoir, I learned everything has to be about *two* things. Along the way, I learned that having too many writing projects at once is *not* appealing to the muse; it's slutty, and she has Standards.

Writing a book is exactly like love. You don't hold back. You give it everything you have. If it doesn't work out, you're heartbroken, but you move forward and start again anyway. You have to.

You don't hold some of yourself in reserve. It's all or nothing. There are no guarantees. If one book doesn't work out, you figure out why. How can you do things differently next time? If you hold back from the book, it won't fully reveal itself. You write each book, utterly and completely giving yourself to it. Some will end up under the bed, sure. And some just might end up brilliant.

ON YOUR PAGE: *Exercise 3*

List twenty-five books you could write. Then set the timer—you have only fifteen minutes to get *something* down for each book concept. For example: Sinter Klaus is number one. What else? What about a book from the perspective of an unusual historical figure? That's a series that could probably go to twenty-five. If you want to write about your family, associate a whole story with each character in your extended cast—every relative gets a novel. For each item, write a title (even if it's silly) and a few words of description. Work fast. The books can be terrible, terrible ideas.

If you're stuck, pretend you've been chosen to receive a special grant that pays your current salary on the condition that you write every day. In order to receive the grant, you have to turn in your list of twenty-five books by the end of the day. What would be your life's work? What kinds of books would you write? Remember: If you are trying to come up with *really good* ideas, you won't likely be able to get into the flow. Get your bad ideas down on paper so you don't have to spend years working on them. Or worse, *thinking* about them.

Chapter 4

The Book 100

If you're serious about writing a book, you would be well served to create a wide plank—a kind of gentle ramp—from your life as it is now into the world of the Writer At Work. This pathway is paved with—can you guess?—books.

Other books.

Reading.

Before you write, and/or during the first phase of your book-writing endeavor, you should read one hundred books *like the one you are intending to write.* I call this the Book 100.

The Pilates exercise system has a basic daily abdominal exercise called the Pilates 100. This move, performed while you lie on your back with your legs in the air and your torso curled in a sustained sit-up, requires you to flap your arms up and down one hundred times. "Like your palms are hammering nails!" my teacher always says as we puff and flap, squeezing our ribs together and sucking in our stomachs.

The Book 100 is much, much more pleasurable: Read one hundred books like the one you want to complete. That's one hundred romance novels, or one hundred literary novels, or one hundred how-to books, or one hundred picture books, or one hundred experimental-hybrid-hard-to-describe books. For children's book authors, this is superbly fun and obviously not that difficult. Novelists and nonfiction biographers are allowed to skim.

Read books from other centuries, other countries, works

in translation. (It's not cheating to count your Wise Guides as part of your Book 100—see chapter 16. And, if you rely on history, research, inspirational, or how-to books to write your book, count up to twenty-five of those.)

The point is to read many, many examples of what you're trying to do. If you can't find one hundred books that are at least a little bit like yours, you might want to reconsider your book idea. Have a serious heart-to-heart with yourself and a few people in the writing business to check out the validity and salability of your dream book. Why aren't there any others? Have you defined your project too narrowly? Is it too weird? You may want to attend a few conferences and test your idea on professionals in the field. You might want to change it.

If you feel daunted and overwhelmed when you hear a suggestion like "Read one hundred books," you're not alone. Adopt the mental attitude of a long-distance runner or other high achiever. Reading one hundred books helps you to build the discipline to stay committed to one thing, one long-term goal, for a long time. (*You can do it!*) When you think about the marathon itself, about actually writing an entire book, notice the rush of fear that quakes your stomach. (*Very normal.*) Take as long as you need to finish your Book 100. Do it with a friend or writing partner, and divide the work in half.

Surround yourself with books. A hundred well-chosen books act as your base camp, your buffer, your personalized M.F.A. writing program. Use the library, use interlibrary loan, use books on tape. Notice what you like and what you love. Writers learn more from reading than from all the how-to-plot books in the world. Like kids learning how to speak, writers internalize the grammar of plot, the shape of the narrative arc, the way dialogue is done well or poorly; you can learn everything about writing from seeing how other people do it.

Reading one hundred books can take a whole year or longer and is best done in advance of your book-writing project, but with some overlap so the books actually take you into the writing. The object is, after all, to *immerse yourself in the book project* for a long enough period of time that you will stay with the thing until it is finished. You will hit a point—after your fifty-second romance novel—where you can't wait another minute! You *have* to start.

Read like a writer, sitting up, not in bed. Pen in hand, note cards, stickies. You're trolling for techniques. You're noticing the plot. You're asking questions: *Why did she start the second chapter here? How does he end his chapters? Why is this introduced on page one?* You're an active little reader, a busy, nosy thing. You aren't reading for pleasure. It should feel like work.

Track your titles and authors so that on down the road, when you're working on the middle of the middle chapter and you flash on that swamp scene in the middle of the middle of—*What was that book?*—you can tickle through your file and recover the tome you need.

There are more benefits to this core workout. For instance, you will become, after reading seventy-five or so books, an expert in this genre. Your ability to write cover letters, speak to agents, give classroom talks about your book when it comes out, will be enhanced, professional, and smart. You'll be informed. In order to court the attention of a publisher, your manuscript needs to kick butt—and you do, too! Publishers invest in writers who can sell books. Knowing your field—depth and breadth wise—gives you that platform to stand on. You'll be able to explain where your book comes from, compare it to others in its class, state how it differs, what it adds. You can't really make this kind of stuff up; it will form the bones of your query, proposal, or cover letter to publishing professionals in the field.

When you join the community of published authors, you become part of a web, a tradition. You might feel like an isolated genius, undiscovered in boring old Cincinnati, but you aren't. You're part of a lively, bright group of actively reading literary people. You have to know what the heck you are doing. You need to say, "This is my address. This is how we live. This is who came before." You are walking in footsteps whenever you write a book, whether you're conscious of it or not.

To prepare for writing *Chapter After Chapter*, I reread the great creative writing guides: Anne Lamott's *Bird by Bird*, Stephen King's *On Writing*, Natalie Goldberg's *Writing Down the Bones*, and several books by the creativity coach Julia Cameron. I reread Eudora Welty's amazing *One Writer's Beginnings*, which prompted me to consider how our ideas about who gets to be a book writer and who doesn't are set forth in earliest childhood. I reread Jerome Stern's *Making Shapely Fiction* and remembered the year he was working on that book and I was his student, and how he tried out chapters on us, which prompted me to do the same with my students and *Chapter*.

I looked at guides for other kinds of artists and fell in love with the approach Frederick Franck uses in *Zen Seeing, Zen Drawing*, the way he weaves stories about the moments he had breakthroughs in seeing with drawings and techniques.

And I didn't just read current creative writing guides. I reconsidered Percy Lubbock's excellent 1957 guide, *The Craft of Fiction*, and Brenda Ueland's *If You Want to Write* from 1938. I went all the way back to the original creative writing manual by Aristotle titled *On Poetry and Style*. In all of these books, a constant theme emerged: Your writing career develops your values, your personal integrity, your confidence, your bravery.

During your 100, will you think, at times, *There is no point in writing another book like this one*? Sure. But you will think this anyway, whether or not you read one hundred books, and the advantages of reading widely are too great. Will you feel that there are lots of bad books out there? Yes. You will feel that anyway, too. You want to be an informed reader. These books, like these fears, *exist*. You need to know them firsthand so you can make your book the best it can be.

I think it's freeing to know that everything has been said before. Fortunately, humans forget wisdom quickly. We have to keep repeating our best messages; we have to pass along the stuff we know. The Book 100 is the best teacher I have ever had. If you're already working on your book, layer in your 100. It's what you can do when you hit the writing wall. If you're hedging on the high dive, ready but not ready to take the plunge, begin, absolutely, with your 100. You will slide into the warm waters of your book project—nothing works better than this.

ON YOUR PAGE: *Exercise 4*

What books do you need to read? Make your list of one hundred titles (remember, some can be how-to, background, research, inspiration). The list is important: You will use it later when you write your proposal for editors and agents. Take your time doing this.

Then start reading. Just work down the list. Give yourself plenty of time—most people need at least a year to read one hundred books. Of course you will skip some, substitute others. New books will be published that you have to add. You can do this before, during, or after you officially start writing your book.

Don't read as a reader. You're not going to have to talk about the books you're reading, teach from them, remember their plots, or look up biographical information on the authors. Read as a writer. Make a little note card (see sample below) for each book you read, and keep the cards in a file. You can skip making cards for books that don't interest you. You're simply making the cards as reminders so that if you need to see a certain technique you can get back to that book without too much trouble.

Title of book:

Book in a sentence (just to remember it):

Book in a paragraph (pretend it's your book and you're explaining it to an agent who has just asked you, "What's your book about?"):

Best thing about this book:

List of memorable, useful techniques (like "great sex scene, page 67"; "good dialogue between the children, page 8"):

Advanced version: The Book 100, like the exercises in your workout class, has modifications—enhancements you can add to push yourself further as you build up confidence and abdominal strength.

- Network by sending letters to your favorite living authors on your 100, telling them what you adore most about their books.
- Learn how to plan and build your book by looking at a few examples of *great* books. Take them apart and analyze them to see how they are put together.
- Give yourself short assignments on days you do not feel like writing: *For one page, imitate the style of Author No. 67 on the list.* It's like learning new dance steps by standing on a great dancer's feet. You'll absorb new moves. Your range will broaden.

Chapter 5

Slow Is Fearless

WHEN YOU ARE AFRAID, WHAT DO YOU DO? RUN?

Most people, when they are feeling anxious, speed up. They scrunch their eyes and hunker down and duck and dive through the situation and hope for the best. A moving target is hardest to hit, right?

If you're nervous about the amount of time and sacrifice a book project takes, your first impulse is more likely *rush* and less likely *take a year to read.* To actively, carefully, intentionally read and study. When you have limited time, your impulse may be: *But I have to get it done sooner—I don't have time to read one hundred books, I don't have three years to write a stupid book, I don't have that kind of time!*

There is only one "kind" of time.

The moment you are in right now. Staying in the now is essentially a kind of fearless focus.

It takes gallons of courage to *slow down.*

In sex, in parenting, in listening to a friend, in caring for an aged person, in gardening, on the freeway—slowing down is really, really good.

We live in a world where it's become a talent, a lost art, something we have to relearn: *Slow down.*

Book authors regularly use speed like a drug. Because we are terrified—of failing, of wrecking up the first draft, of telling the truth, of sucking, of pretty much everything that has anything to do with writing a book—we rush.

When I am incredibly nervous that I have nothing to say, nothing at all, and that it was wrong—completely, totally, fantastically wrong—for an editor to take a chance on me, for my book proposal to have been purchased (*What were they, blind? Stupid? I can't write books!*), I start to do this weird incremental rushing thing. It's gradual, so I haven't been able to notice it quickly enough to nip it in the bud. The last time this happened, it wasn't until my editor wrote me an eight-page single-spaced letter that ended by saying, "If you need more time, like another year, to finish this book, we can make that happen. You just need to let me know."

Oh.

Big breakthrough, lights flashing on all over the house, giant realization. *How did I not see this?*

Rushing blinds you to the obvious. Rushing comes from fear and is designed to keep you from looking down into the canyon and seeing how tenuous your perch on the wire is. Rushing is a survival skill. It's really old. It helps your body get through hard situations. *Go, go, go, go, go, go, go!* the brain tells the body. Chemicals course through your veins. *Book deadline? Whoooooooooooooooooosh, go. Go, go, go, go, go. If you work hard and fast, it will get done!*

So not.

So badly done.

Writing too fast, wanting too much too soon, is writing scared.

A lot of people I know write too fast. They're the opposite of the I-can't-start-I'm-stuck people. It's the same thing manifested differently.

Fight: The scared writer person is in this wrestling match with himself, locked.

Or flight: The scared writer person is running super fast, hoping people will say he's brilliant and fast! But really he's just spinning his wheels.

Both of these states are likely to visit you.

The solution is to pay attention to how fear manifests itself in your body. When I first learned about this, I thought it was the stupidest, most touchy-feely goofball therapy in the world. I resisted mightily. *Notice how my body feels? In order to write? Take the time to get inside the feeling-body, the mind-body? Give me a break.*

Then, I read about Slow Food.

Food I understand. Food and body = I am there.

So, there is a movement, started in Italy (where else), devoted to all things that take an enormous amount of time. A reaction to McDonald's, Burger King, hyper-this and super-speedy-that, the Slow Food Movement embraces artisanal bread, old vine wines, meals that take hours to consume because each bite is savored, and the conversation is the most valuable dish served.

The Slow Food people like bicycles, beaches, books, and face-to-face meetings. They do not believe in gyms (though there is a super-slow weight-lifting wing to the movement—try it. Slow-lifting is incredibly hard and very effective!), cell phones, or cities in particular. The Slow Foodies like locally grown food, sustainable living, and slow activities: walking, knitting, cooking, and talking.

But the Slow Food Movement is not "a charter for slackers and born-again beatniks," according to one Harvard professor. Selective slowness—choosing what things to do and giving yourself more time to do them—is just plain common sense.

Writing, just like the Slow Food Movement, is countercultural to our speedy ways of life.

Writing is slow. Always has been.

Writing books is, and should be, *really* slow.

The great books are still around—just like the great recipes, the great songs, the great trees—*because they took a long time to develop.*

Slow is good. Slow is great.

Slow is the new fast.

If you are looking for a shortcut, a way to multitask and write your book, I urge you to be dubious of any method that promises you a good quality manuscript quickly.

You can taste the difference between quick bread and bread that went through two rises, just as you can sense the difference in books, articles, and television scripts that were written too fast and those that steeped, incubated, went through good, nurturing rewrites.

Time-soaked writing is good writing.

When I published my collection of poetry, I gathered poems I had been working on over a period of ten years. They were *steeped.* And I think—I hope—deeper for it.

While some individual pieces may come fast, almost whole, born on the page easily, books take a long time to pull together. You will, perhaps, but not always, have some great sections that come quickly. But all the writing you do to link those sections—that's going to take months. It's supposed to. A book is a living, thinking, breathing, alive thing. You can make a pizza in a couple hours, but not a book.

Slow is good for the alchemy—the rise—of words and ideas and imagination and emotion. Good things are slow. Slow, slow, slow.

You need to take your time.

Get it? Take *your* time?

Your writing session, your writing year, your writing life, must be padded, anchored, and illuminated with time to wander, get off track, launch a different writing project, lose yourself in reading, write for no purpose, just to explore. You need leisure writing, reading, walking. You need to play. And you need solitude that is not writing time, too.

All these hours have to be factored in.

Think of your favorite authors. Think of the great pieces of writing you turn to again and again. How many truly stunning books in your favorite category do you find in a year? A lifetime? Books take years, not months. My favorite authors publish a single book every five to twenty years.

Can you double the amount of time you are giving yourself to become a writer? Can you soften your whole approach and try to move past that fight/flight response to writing anxiety? What if you let your writing apprenticeship—the part where you learn—take two years? Five? Ten?

You can write when you are old, you know.

Can your deadline for getting this book *done, done, done* (you have many internal deadlines, whether you are conscious of them or not) be made more realistic to accommodate the true shape of your writing life?

What is your hurry about? Are you rushing because you want to make money off your books, so you feel you must crank them out? If so, it might be worth slowing down and designing your product (which you can then replicate quickly) so that it is of the highest quality you are capable of making. Are you rushing because of fear? Are you scared of failing? Are you writing Band-Aid style, ripping through your writing life, determined not to feel any pain?

Rushed things—days, sewing projects, workouts, weddings, rehearsals—are time wasted. You hurry, but you don't get anywhere, nothing important or good happens. Books *can't* be rushed. Art making is a natural process. Nature has rules. Nine months to make a baby. Two years, perhaps, to make a book. Complex projects—and books *always* are—need time to cook.

American farm-raised salmon are genetically modified to reach maturity six times faster than nature intended. Fertilizer, growth hormones, factory farms, super-pesticides—our food is on the fast track to the table. This food is fast, and it's cheap, standardized, tasteless, and possibly unhealthy. "Two centuries ago," Carl Honore wrote in his book *In Praise of Slowness*, "the average pig took 5 years to reach 130 pounds; today it hits 220 after just 6 months and is slaughtered before it loses its baby teeth."

This is too fast.

The last book I drafted read like farm-fed growth hormone weirdness. I was running all over the place. Writing it, it *felt* good. Productive. I can type 137 words a minute, no mistakes. But writing isn't typing.

Writing takes time, and the conveniences of these modern times—broadband, wireless, podcasting, voice-recognition software—do not speed up or even aid the writing process.

I do not have the Internet or e-mail hooked up in the room where I do my writing. I stay away from anything associated with "high-speed access." The access I want comes from low, slow connections to real stuff, ideas in old books, old people, bicycles, four-hour dinners, seasonal change.

It's your relationship to speed and your ability to observe your anxiety, to discern when those two forces are protecting you from doing your best work, providing a drug-like illusion that you are mighty and powerful!

Are you, like so many new and experienced writers I know, constantly berating yourself for not writing more, for not having started sooner, not finishing pieces, not being published yet, wasting your time? If so, you are quite possibly internalizing cultural tendencies—this inexorable push for speediness at the cost of quality.

Writing is supposed to be slow.

It's supposed to take a long time.

Instead of resisting slow, lean into it. Get accustomed to it.

Do you need to bring more slow things into your life, slower music, slower reading, harder books, slower pace of life, fewer activities?

Speed is usually fear. Find out for yourself.

ON YOUR PAGE: *Exercise 5*

Keep a "slow notebook" this week. Use simple paper and, of course, a pencil, which makes you write more slowly than a pen. What kinds of things take time to do well? Beautiful handmade furniture by that guy your husband knows? Wooden canoes? Walking in the dunes? Your mom's good stew? Your four-year-old daughter's really, really long stories at bedtime? Best friendships? Notice what happens when you speed up. Notice what happens when you intentionally slow down.

Writers move at a pace different from the rest of society in order to notice things. Take an act you usually perform fast—shaving, washing, dishes, driving—and slow way, way, way down to the point of absurdity. If you usually have a one-hour lunch on Saturday with your mom, give yourself two hours. What do you see? What's different? Write in your notebook what you notice.

Then, make a new plan (in your head or on paper) that *doubles* the amount of time you have given yourself to write your book. Double or triple everything: the amount of time you deserve to spend reading other books, revising your work, learning the etiquette and protocols of the publishing world, going to conferences, networking with writers, entering the literary community, attending readings and book signings. Grant yourself *acres* of time, and notice how your body feels.

Chapter 6
Alone Together

WOLVES AND DOGS RANGE ACROSS STEPPES AND TOWNS, AND they often *look* like they are all alone. But they have a keen sense of where everyone is—especially other canines—and what those other dogs are doing.

Writers are the same way.

Ours is work we do alone yet also together.

When writing a book, you are (whether or not you actively participate) in a pack of other book writers. You're writing alone in your studio for hundreds of hours, yet you're writing to an audience—maybe millions of people—and at any given moment, writers all over the world are writing alongside you, alone in *their* studios. You're surrounded, all the time, and behind you is a literary history—thousands of characters and authors who've gone before you on this very path.

Writing can't be done alone. You need other people to make it happen: early readers, editors, book designers, book buyers, bookstore owners, reviewers, people who fall in love with *your* book. Writing a book is like building a house or birthing a child or starting a company. Maybe you could do it completely alone in total isolation. But why would you want to? And how healthy would it be, really?

In a pack, we learn how to be better writers when we're on our own, and we hone our group skills by socializing through our work. To form, maintain, feed, and steer a good, productive writing group is an art not unlike that of actually writing a book. It's good work, and a good use of your time (better than Bunco!) to practice working in a group.

Writing groups help us to communicate our ideas effectively, maintain momentum and confidence, learn more about the marketplace, discover books to put on your Book 100 list, get feedback on chapters, and get help with query and cover letters. The writing group votes on our author photo proofs and takes us out to dinner when our book is accepted. We do our best work when we are connected, viscerally, with a tidy pack of friendly wolves, dogs who run at about the same pace, some a little faster, stronger, older, wiser, others coming up through the ranks, but all committed to the same seriousness of purpose: Writing books.

Just as you have several families in your life—your work family, your friends-who-are-like-family, your in-laws, your family of origin—you may need different writing partners or groups for different purposes. I have Debra and Jackie for work on poetry. Anne and Janis for novels. Lorraine and Anne and Steve and Sarah are my tight late-night memoir pack. And they all have other packs, too. Lorraine has her short story hounds; Debra ranges around with her formal poetry people and her feral wild poets, and these two packs never cross paths.

Groups live and change and die. New dogs show up and fit right in. Old dogs fall away. A group ending isn't a failure—it's the end of a natural life cycle. You'll have "under-the-bed" groups—it's part of the learning process. Some just won't work out. Sometimes you are in a group in order to learn more about how groups work (and do not work).

When one group ends, move on quickly. That's not failure. It's learning. Big difference.

Don't stay in a group that isn't helping your writing. Avoid groups that are (1) more interested in wine or whining than writing; (2) more interested in discussing reading books than writing; or (3) more interested in gossiping and being jealous of other writers than commenting on works-in-progress. Be careful of groups that have lots of people who have "ideas" for books but aren't actively working on a book.

If your group isn't working and you want to save it, you have three choices: (1) bring in a consultant—a guest writer to demonstrate new ways of working; (2) have a group caucus and work through a new mission statement for more clarity, allied expectations, and increased focus; or (3) quit. Too many people stay in groups out of some weird sense of social obligation. You don't have time for that! Plus, you're hurting more people than you're helping by enabling a nonfunctioning entity.

When I first began working in groups, I didn't realize they had a life cycle. I thought your writing group was like your marriage—you stayed in it for the long haul. I've worked with Anne for nearly twenty years and Janis for fifteen. But groups do have a life cycle. They aren't marriages. They're business propositions; when they aren't profitable anymore, you start up a new business, reinvesting your capital wisely.

When one group ends, another forms. Writers move toward each other, in supportive, helpful ways.

I used to be in a fabulous group, the Spunky Monkeys. I thought we would last forever. For almost three years, we met once every two weeks on Friday afternoons at Jack's house to trade poems. Each of us was working on a book manuscript, and every time we met, we each brought a new poem. Sometimes, we worked on revisions from the last session's work. We shared calls for poetry, Web sites, magazines, journals, and other things that were helpful to the writers in the group. "I heard *Controlled Burn* wants Michigan poets for its upcoming issue." "Did you see the feature on Van Jordan in *Poets & Writers?* I copied it for you, Jane, in case you missed it." We spent equal time on each poem. We didn't eat or drink alcohol or complain about the poetry world, and we didn't talk about teaching, students, spouses, or home renovations. Each session lasted two to three hours. Because of these group guidelines and our uninterrupted focus, it was a great group, very productive.

Then I fell in love with a man from another town, and I needed Friday afternoons to get to him. And so I missed a bunch of sessions. Right around then, a publisher fell in love with Greg's poems, and Greg published his book. Then Jack moved to a new house on the other side of town, and Jane retired. The group ended—though some of us met in various "doubles" for a while. There were no hard feelings; there was no drama. The Monkeys had just, like a plant or any living thing, run its life cycle.

The longer you're in a group, though, the better you'll get at being part of a group, and the more you'll benefit and contribute. You'll get better at giving feedback, and you'll become better at incorporating what is helpful and what is not.

Your group is your writing family. The more you learn about working with others on a creative project at the earliest stages of the work, the better the life of the book later. It's not just about improving your manuscript. It's about your literary citizenship, the way you become a part of the writing world. In order to be a good writer who works well with sales reps and publishers and agents and audiences, you need good group skills.

Most writers aren't social butterflies. Introversion, weirdness, disability, isolation, social criticism, distaste for large festive gatherings, alienation from family and clubs—these are hallmarks of the writing personality. If you have struggled with groups—finding a good one, feeling comfortable and trusting, being useful in one—you're like most writers. We're weird. We're awkward and sensitive. We don't thrive in social settings. But what grown-up writers do—what real book writers do—is to construct a self that Plays Well With Others. They maintain strict boundaries around the isolated, tormented, party-hating, writer-genius self. When they leave the house for writing group, they have a "how can I serve" mentality. *How can I help the whole group—this pack I run with—be the best little writing posse east of the Rockies?*

For many of us, becoming this professional, social, confident, gives-great-feedback person takes a good deal of stretching and not a little faking it. The creativity it takes for you to allow these parts of yourself to come to the fore *is exactly the kind of confidence you need to finish your book.* If you're stretching yourself, working through your discomfort, dreaming up ways to work well with others, you're working on your book. If you're resenting, gossiping, being jealous, worrying about how clean your house is, or drinking too much, you're taking energy away from your book.

So the point is: Be normal. Act like a normal person would *in a business setting.* A writing group is more like a board meeting and less like a cocktail party. Tortured writers often write beautifully and a lot. But they won't get publishing contracts if they're too difficult to work with.

Before, during, and after the Spunky Monkeys, I had and continue to have my own private writing partner, Janis, who lives in Texas. We exchange novel chapters regularly. When we're actively working on a book, we e-mail ten new pages to each other every Friday morning at 5 A.M. and discuss them at 7 A.M. via telephone. Now that her draft is circulating with publishers and I'm working on other projects, we touch base with a phone call every week. We read each other's cover letters and query drafts. I send her books to read, and she does the same for me. When reading trade journals and browsing Web sites, we keep an eye out for the names of editors and agents we think the other would like. We keep the relationship alive, making a little company of Writers at Work.

You're allowed to have more than one writing partner; it's not cheating, it's *productive.* Just as you have your walking partner, your cycling friends, and your swim mate, you can have different kinds of people reading your work. Beginning just this last fall, I also now trade work with Lorraine, who works in several different genres. She has a new young adult novel out, and she's working on a second collection of short stories and a novel. Lorraine is one of the best readers I have ever had. I have to really work on my game to keep up with her; asking her if we could trade was one of the bravest, hardest things I have ever done. (It was easier, post divorce, to ask out a guy, and that was just about impossible.)

I met Lorraine at a reading (this is one reason you are urged to attend literary readings and writing conferences—to find tennis partners, packs to run with!). She doesn't say what's good or bad, she *reads* the work and tells me what I am doing, how it is to read it, what happens to her inside her head on many, many levels. Lorraine, in her letters to me about my drafts, draws from her dream book, Freud, the Bible, a dictionary of myths—reading a Lorraine letter is like attending a fabulous lecture at an Ivy League school, tailor-made just for you. I feel completely inept in her presence and I love Lorraine with my heart and soul. Do I deserve Lorraine? I don't know. I have been yearning for a Lorraine to read my work my whole life. I'm lucky, for certain. But I have also read a lot of manuscripts, no charge, for a lot of people. I believe helping other writers as generously as you can is a good way to open the doors for your Lorraine.

You must trust your instincts. You should be, in a good group, a tiny bit nervous—at first—because you want to do a good job, to be smart and helpful. Then, you should settle into a good working rhythm. It's okay to feel some envy when others in the group publish or win prizes or finish faster. You can express your delight wholeheartedly and also say quietly, "I hope that happens to me soon, too." You should feel pushed and challenged but never teased or diminished. You should feel you are *working hard* but never giving away more than you are receiving. It's a lot to continually monitor and learn. All groups will have flaws, blah sessions, words that shouldn't have been said, screwups, off days, a few misses. There are annoying wolves in all packs. I have heard some writers complain bitterly about how bad their writing group is. "Why are you in it?" I want to say. "You can quit."

The time you spend in the group should generate *exponentially more writing time for you.* Having a deadline to bring in your new work is essential. Otherwise, perhaps the time commitment—reading all the other people's work—is not worth it. You do learn a lot that you will apply, unconsciously, to your own writing from having to articulate how a piece of writing works and doesn't work. But the group needs to be small enough and meet often enough (Every two weeks? Every week? Once a month?) for each person in the group to get regular feedback.

The writing group is your glorious dress rehearsal.

When you're writing, working from the inside, it's vital that you come up for air, that you connect with other people. The inside of your head is completely and utterly dark. If you stay in there and never come out you can get very lost, very off-track. You need constant, regular check-ins with normal, healthy people. They are your lanterns.

Choosing good people to work with is a process. It might take time to get the right group together. Stay open-minded and don't invest time in groups that aren't as serious as you are. Those people can become your lunch buddies or tennis partners. Interview people by agreeing to trade work with them just once. You'll have chemistry with a few people, and that is all you need.

A small focused pack of wolves, lone individuals who work solo but also together. Howling for joy.

ON YOUR PAGE: *Exercise 6*

Develop a roster. Make a list of every person you could contact to find a writing partner or writing group. Teachers of creative writing at colleges within a hundred miles of you. Online sites. The presidents of the various writing organizations in your state. People you have met at writing conferences. Acquaintances from high school or college who might be writing. Who are your smartest friends? Remember, you need people who are *writing something like what you're writing*.

Work on a two- to three-sentence description of yourself and your project. This is always harder than it seems! What's the nature of your experience? At what point are you in your project? What kind of partner(s) are you looking for? Jot down what amounts to a personal ad, and send it to three people on your roster. For instance:

> Writer, mid-fifties, BA in English, 1972 from Smith, seeks writing partner(s) for motivation, feedback, support, insight. If you are interested in working through a course of exercises from _____ (book) by ________(author), meeting weekly or biweekly, and you plan to begin your novel this year, please call. Literary or genre authors; novels only.

Chapter 7

Surround Sound

NON-BOOK WRITERS (AND CERTAIN SUPER-ORGANIZED people who are clever compartmentalizers) believe that book writing can be tucked in around the edges of a life, an add-on, a hobby. Something you whip out, on the side, while remaining a productive member of society.

I suppose there are people who write quietly and neatly, their books appearing with no big drama. But most people, especially on their first book, struggle with a terrible insidious mental weed called Creep. If you don't surround yourself with your book, you risk it creeping away from you—or you unintentionally creeping away from it. Creep is bad, and it's as common as the common cold.

The book writers I know all live, eat, breathe, and sleep *the book*. Or … they're trying to get back to the place where they live, eat, breathe, and sleep *the book.* This complete absorption in the project is desirable, to be courted. To reach this level of concentration, of focus, though, you have to set up your book-writing life so you're never too far away from the project. This is the only way to prevent Creep from overtaking your project.

Think of writing a book as like buying one of those speaker systems that envelop you in sound. No matter where you are, *you are surrounded*. Similarly, you must allow the book you're writing to wrap itself around you and permeate every single part of your life. Your book should always be running in the background of your mind, even when you aren't literally putting words on paper in your studio.

Of course, at the outset, being into the book is very much like falling in love—it's easy. The book thinks about you, you can't not think about the book, you obsess about each other, you rush to your writing sessions. You're crazy about each other and always willing to drop everything to see one another.

But some time after you make a real and public commitment to each other, doubt sets in. Annoyance. It gets difficult! You may feel shackled. You feel like you chose the wrong book. The book has flaws. The flaws annoy the heck out of you. The book gets gassy! It's terrible—there are parts of the book that stink. You get sick of the book. The book is needy. Sometimes, though you would never say it out loud, you think, *Screw the book.* And you are wracked with shame. *Other books wouldn't be so demanding*, you think. *Wasn't I happier before I was in this relationship?*

Here is the secret to writing a book: Find a way to keep your desire alive and pure.

Talent is desire.

Those who want to write their books the most end up writing them, and those who only have good intentions may or may not. To keep yourself *wanting* to write the book sometimes requires cheering yourself on. There's a part of you (maybe dormant, but it's there) that is a goofy, hyperactive, wildly enthusiastic cheerleader. Sometimes you have to call on her: *You can do it! You want it! Go Author!* And let her rip. Other times, you might have to make an actual list of all the reasons why you really want to do this book; the reasons not to write are going to bop into your life on an hourly basis. *Talent is desire* means you practice blocking out the negatives while courting the positives. It means sending flowers to your book—metaphorical or real—from the author part of you regularly.

And desire is stoked and invigorated by constant and prolonged exposure to the book.

My friend Connie has a master of fine arts in writing. She's a teacher and an avid reader. She has published a few short stories, and she wants to write a novel. She has *started* lots of novels—six that she can think of off the top of her head: two coming-of-age novels, two she's got opening chapters for, and two middle-age-people-having-affairs novels. She's had some dalliances, too. That novel in poems she was going to write. The blockbuster romance. Those fizzled pretty fast.

Connie decided that last summer was her time to *really* write the book. She set up a schedule—8 A.M to 12 P.M.—and she posted it on her family's fridge. She did great on the first three mornings in June. She was having the total surround sound experience. She thought about her characters while she was in the grocery store, picking out onions. She overhead dialogue at the oil change place that *had* to go in the book—it was perfect! She dreamed about the book, woke up thinking about the book, and everything was good. For three days in a row, she wrote, and for three nights in a row dinner was on the table, and the kids were normal (the real-life kids).

Then, on day four she had to take her daughter to the dentist.

Dr. Oppenheimer.

Who really does seem to hate her daughter.

So there was a lot of anxiety that morning. And Connie didn't think about the book. Or the characters. She thought about Dr. Oppenheimer. *Why were they doing braces, really? Why was orthodontia marketed so aggressively to kids?* She thought a lot about writing a letter to the editor on this topic. Or an article. A whole book.

Then a bunch of other real-life stuff happened involving aging parents, the neighbor, a bad headache, and an exploding vacuum cleaner.

Connie missed three days of writing.

The surround sound turned off.

The book was in her writing room, on her desk. Still alive.

Just barely.

Humming so softly, you would at this point have needed special equipment in order to hear the heartbeat, to pick up the tune. Very, very faintly, Connie's tender new book was still there.

You have to allow the book to wrap itself around you. All the time. Everywhere you go. Your mind needs to be turning it over, chewing it, stirring it, working it. All the time, in the back of your mind.

The dreaded Creep is always out there, slowly trying to steal your book from you.

You know how your house is sinking into the earth? Except you don't really see it because it's happening so slowly? That's how it is to get away from your book. Creep is subtle. You may not notice it until *years have gone by!* This is very common even though it sounds so drastic. Sometimes it really does take years to notice that you quit something. Even if you really loved that something.

The only antidote: surround sound. Never turn off the stereo.

One visit to Dr. Oppenheimer and *whoosh* your stereo implodes. You don't get back to your novel that day, or the next day, or the next, and you don't even know what happened, or that anything at all happened!

And that's what happened to Connie last summer.

Because she missed writing on Thursday, it was harder to start on Friday—she'd lost her thread. Surround sound had been turned off, and she didn't even notice! She could sort of hear the *I should write* voice, that nagging buzz. But it was a "should," not the loving lure of the book itself.

Then her Saturday was filled with family stuff. "Write from 9 A.M. to 12 P.M." was on her calendar, but then *she wrote over it in pen:* "Go shopping for dryer, soccer shoes, vacuum, card for Steketees." These things were written over the sacred writing hours like graffiti, and Connie didn't even think much about it. And she didn't think much about not thinking about it.

In fact, it didn't occur to her to make up the missed work, the absent hours. By Sunday, Connie wasn't thinking about her book at all.

If you do not take the book with you everywhere you go, keeping it alive and thriving in your mind's eye, if you don't nurture it and anticipate its needs, the book will creep away from you. It has to be always on. If you abandon the book, even for a few hours, it may leave you.

On a Monday, a full ten days later, Connie got up and went to her desk at 8 A.M. to write—back on her program, no problem. She still thought of herself as a novel writer, but she felt overwhelmed and defeated, and she didn't even know why, exactly. It just seemed so *hard* to write a novel. She got mad at herself and thought, *Why do I think I can write a book?* (A soul-killing anti-book thought that can cause you to lose an entire year.)

Connie bagged writing that day and decided to use her sacred time to read, and then, feeling like a failure, she napped, and then she got an early lunch (she was starving), and then she felt like a fat failure. It was a terrible day!

You can't take your eyes off the book. Not for very long, anyway. You must stay surrounded. Happily.

Court surround sound, and write your book from within that shimmering envelope. Fight Creep with intention. Tether yourself to the book every day. When you notice it slipping away, turn up the volume on your writing life. All the way to ten.

ON YOUR PAGE: *Exercise 7*

Make a list of twenty little assignments—things that trigger you to think about some aspect of your book. Then place each assignment, each Creep Emergency Antidote, on its own card and stick one card in your glove box, planner, desk drawer, nightstand, lunch box, mirror.

Some examples from my desk:

- Write Alyssa conversation from evening at the park.
- Write passage on running with the New York group and face-recognition issues.
- Make a list of twenty-five potential titles.
- Make a working table of contents.

- Read the draft from start to finish.
- Put key scenes on note cards and hang over desk.

As your work on the book continues to deepen, your little assignments will become more specific.

For example, today I "programmed" my surround sound system to play tunes that would help me think of people I know who have written books. Just a kind of general way of working on this project. So that during the day, authors would pop up, people I could interview. Tomorrow, I'll have a different intention. And different little assignments.

Chapter 8
Positioning

JUST AS CHILDREN COLLECT THEIR BOOKS AND LAY OUT THEIR gear the night before school to make the next day's start a little easier, purposeful book authors also lay out their things, mentally and physically preparing for the next writing day.

My friend Eric, a Pulitzer Prize nominee, calls this process "positioning." He sees himself as the owner of a business, and he's very clear about what needs to happen—about what paper and files are required, and which scenes and sections need to be attended to before noon. Every evening, he makes a list. The whole shape of his writing day is concrete in his mind the night before. Then he relaxes and enjoys dinner with his wife.

Everything is set up for the next day, like dominoes, and in the morning he just has to get his butt to the chair, flick his finger, and the process immediately has its own momentum. Eric can stay on task for several hours. He doesn't always get everything done, but that's okay because that un-done stuff provides the starter, the inspiration, the mother, the liquor, for the next positioning session.

Positioning is a strategy less about organization and more about combating fear and staying focused. This positioning technique is a way to tether yourself to the book-in-progress, leash yourself to the work. A lot of people have a hard time finishing projects because they don't understand how to continue a long sequence of writing days. After a hiatus, they forget their strategies for getting back into the work.

A good writing session has a lot to do with the previous writing session and the period in between. Not finishing is usually related to not focusing, and positioning is how you keep your focus between writing sessions.

Although I didn't know it at the time, I did this nightly preparation when I wrote *Georgia Under Water*, my collection of short stories. I wasn't aware my nightly visits to my studio were a step in the book-writing process, but they were. Before I went to bed each night, I always visited my writing studio. I'd sneak in and place my hands on the file or notes or printed pages or part of the book I was going to work on the next day. I shuffled the papers around, read over the note cards spread out on my little stand. I looked—literally—ahead. Every night, I read over my road map, the outline tacked on my bulletin board. Every night, I traced with my finger exactly where I had been and where I hoped to go the next day.

At the time, I would have felt funny telling you about this nightly round; I would have been embarrassed to be seen in there stroking my printed-out pages, gazing at my note cards. I thought I was going into the room each night just for the thrill of witnessing *forward progress.* That's what I felt when I was in there, like I was making sure what I had written really existed. It was kind of like celebrating each night, and *also like a big fret-fest.* I was scared to go to sleep not knowing where I had left off, without a plan—a loose plan, an intention—for the next day. I didn't make myself do this. I just had to know where I was. I had to know my position.

Writing a book is exactly like traveling in a country you don't know well. What do you do in bed in a new country before you fall asleep? Look at maps. Orient yourself. Memorize the landscape, the roads, the route you will take tomorrow to the post office or pharmacy or castle. You put things together in your head. *Oh, Sienna is to the north! No wonder I have been so confused! It is not near Naples at all.*

Each night, before you go to bed, you need to plant a giant YOU ARE HERE sign in your manuscript and look down the road to see where you might go tomorrow. Realize that, just as in travel, you might change your mind, or the universe might have other plans (thunderstorm, train strike, computer meltdown, handsome new character at breakfast ...).

Nightly visits to your writing space keep you physically *and* subconsciously connected to your book.

Mentally rehearsing (like athletes, actors, and public speakers do all the time) while in your studio space the night before your next writing session deepens and enriches your relationship to your material, heightens your creativity, and increases productivity. "I'll work on the make-out scene in the next chapter." Or, "I'll reread my notes on the history of the battle, and then I'll work on the dialogue between the governor and the chief." Or, "I'll reread my interview with Joe. Then, I want to write Joe's scenes. I need at least three."

Successful book authors have a big plan—*Write novel!*—and a million tiny plans. Book writers throw little hooks forward into the great expanse of the Unwritten to keep themselves on track. They can't sustain the fearless focus that a book requires without figuring out how to keep their minds in the game. This kind of concentration—not the amount of *time* you have—is what finishes books. If laying out your clothes the night before didn't work for you as a kid, and it doesn't work for you now, create your own positioning strategies. Pay attention to how you work and repeat what's effective. It doesn't take much—Eric's positioning sessions last about fifteen minutes; my late-night *Georgia Under Water* visits were only tiny moments, glances, touching base.

I wasn't aware of how I worked when I wrote *Georgia Under Water*. I just wrote. I didn't think anyone would ever read the book (though I desperately hoped and prayed for publication). I do know I was never more than two steps away from that book. I always tell people it came out whole. Which is misleading, maybe even a lie. It didn't come out whole; I kept it whole. I kept it wholly alive the entire three years I drafted it. That's what I really mean. I wrote from *one uninterrupted space* (finishing my Ph.D. and moving twice and getting engaged along the way).

When I wrote my next novel (which turned out to be an under-the-bed project), I worked in the same studio and on the same computer. I'd started on it even before *Georgia* arrived in bookstores. I wanted to follow up with a big bang, a giant success, to move from a small press to a big publisher, get an agent, attend parties, make money. I started the novel in the summer, and my novel-writing partner, Janis, started her book the exact same day. I had no other work responsibilities. All day existed for writing. Evenings were for making elaborate dinners, chatting, gardening. I never went in and checked on the book at night. It never occurred to me to position—I was able to spend eight hours a day writing. I was a Writer. Now that I had the gift of a giant expanse of time—four months with no commitments—I would write a *real* book.

But I was terrified of that second attempt. I was terrified I didn't know what I was doing. I was terrified I would never be able to repeat what I had done before. I was sure *Georgia* had been undeserved, a mistake, a terrible idea. The voice in my head kept saying things like, *I do not deserve to have published my first book. Everyone is watching! This next book has got to be great! People think I am a writer now! I have to pull off this whole trick. I am a fake.*

Never once did it occur to me to get ready for writing the night before. If it had occurred to me to do so—to go into the studio at night and check on my novel, to position—it would have utterly bummed me out. *To do what?* I didn't want to face that novel. Especially after I sent it to Janis in August and she said, "Well, uh. Hmm. I'm not sure I believe these characters. Do you know them? Do you even like them, Heather?"

It never occurred to me to tend to them, to buy into their story, to live inside it. I was pushing the novel uphill from 8 A.M. to 3 P.M. every day. When I didn't *have* to be in that writing room, I was as far away as I could get.

Everything was hollow and weird; I didn't know *how* I had done it the first time. And I was scared if I found out how, I wouldn't be able to do it again. I was scared my writing life was a fluke. And the less I knew about how it worked, the better.

It's only now, ten years later, that I can look back and see what really was. I worked incredibly hard on my first book. Day after day after day. I read voraciously. I worked on each story so intently. I just kept shaping them, reading them aloud to myself, and going back in—learning more and more about the process by simply doing it.

Why didn't that work the second time, for the dreadful mother-daughter novel? On the surface, it looked like I was doing the same things—working hard, focusing, staying with it. But I never let that book into my heart. I never let it take over my life. I never fully believed in it because I didn't believe in or trust myself, and I was blind to *everything*. A book is like a child. You can't fake it. You can't be terrified all the time, or you'll screw up the kid. You have to at some point say, "Okay. Here's what we will do. I have a plan. Trust me." And you have to say it confidently enough to *convince yourself*.

I took care of my first book manuscript like a new parent does a baby. I checked on it all the time. I practically had a baby monitor in the studio: I left the computer running at night in case I got an idea in my sleep. I *ran* down the hall and into that room—I was never more than two steps away.

The awful second novel was never on my mind, never part of me the way the first one was. I was just the daytime babysitter. I wasn't around at night for the precious, vitally important tuck-in. I was never the parent of that novel. It was something I wanted—this book, written, done, great. I didn't position with that book. I didn't obsess over that book. It's a subtle difference. But my writing plans and intentions never came from deep within the book *itself*. They came from me, a writer on autopilot.

To position, you have to give yourself over to the book, its will, its rules, its demands. You have to lose control in a very controlled, ritualized fashion. The night before, identify a new and mysterious site on the map, and point yourself toward the darkest, most interesting, most unknown place to visit the next day. You pack yourself for the trip.

Failure to set a specific writing intention the night before, and to do so every single night, is one of the reasons books fester inside of us, turn against us, and then slip free from our needy, clingy, distracted grip.

Write safe. Lay out your things the night before. Position your book clearly every single night before you go to sleep. Keep your book close and prepare it for its day. Like you would do for any tiny new thing you love that has a life and mind of its own.

ON YOUR PAGE: *Exercise 8*

In one sitting, create one hundred index cards of tasks for completing this project. Tiny, tiny micro movements—truly ten-minute chunks. For example: "Write the first half of the Joey/April sex scene." "Write a first paragraph." "Write the last paragraph." "Outline chapter twelve." And so forth. Make the cards, and then shuffle the deck. Off you go. Just as if you were giving a caretaker instructions on how you manage your home, write these tasks on the cards as though to a well-meaning but not particularly bright or informed person. (After all, in the face of THE BLANK PAGE, we are all struck dumb.)

In this way, you are teaching yourself how to write your book. Some writers keep making cards like this throughout the writing process—tossing out those that no longer apply during their evening positioning session. You can outline your whole book organically using this method. (If you are a night writer, do your positioning at breakfast or on your lunch hour.)

One caveat: You might be tempted to talk about your plan, to ask others for ideas for your plan. Do not do this. The nightly positioning—the laying out of your things—is a sacred ritual and it has to be kept a secret—only you and the book can know—or it doesn't work. Shh.

Chapter 9

Mike's Mistake

Mike Otten was one of the top writing students in his college's undergraduate writing program. He won major departmental awards for creative writing. His work appeared in the college literary magazine. He'd given several live readings in the community's coffee shops. He had a writing group that met on sofas in an attic of an underused old building on campus. Mike's poems were funny and charming and accessible, about working in restaurants and the lessons that come sideways from difficult customers and bad days. His stories were deft and original. "Kafka meets Bart Simpson, but in a really good way," one student said, describing Mike's latest. We all agreed. Mike's work was as good as the stuff we read in magazines like *Rhino* and *Conduit* and *Alligator Juniper.* Mike confided his dream to the writing group: "I want to write the Great American Novel."

They were a little surprised, but not really. Mike could probably do anything. His stories didn't seem exactly Great American Novelish—they were quirky and experimental and edgy and brief and magical. But whatever. "Go for it!" they said.

And so he did.

But his group didn't know what to say about the first installment. It was so un-Mike, this new writing.

So they said: "We need to see more?" They were very nervous, this group. Mike's writing wasn't Mike-esque; it was ... different. It was like he was trying too hard. His voice was stiff. He was using *adverbs.*

Mike pulled down his funky orange beanie. *Were they intimidated because he was going for his dreams? Did they just like the other stuff? Would they reject anything new he tried? Would he be able to grow in this group?*

Mike continued on, writing each chapter according to his plan, not holding back. This was the Great American Novel; he wanted it to sound worthy and large. He had it all mapped out. It was about a doctor in Africa, adultery, and the patients' new school.

After a few months, the writing group sort of fell apart.

When Mike came to me, he was groupless, stuck in the middle of his untitled two-volume masterwork. He had one question: "How do I get an agent?"

When I saw him, I saw a person *in pieces.*

Literally.

Some of what he knew about writing—the dedication, desire, commitment, high goals—was hanging on to him, but in a kind of tattered way. Other parts had fallen away.

He'd forgotten what he knew, what he practiced when he was a learning writer and not a Great American Novel writer.

This is a common phase we go through when moving from a "writing life" to a "writing books life."

I asked Mike if he felt like maybe he was trying too hard with this novel.

He said, "No." No, he had a plot and a vision—he had the whole thing planned out. He was right on track. He was writing every day.

I pointed to the word "fungible," a word the old Mike would have never used, except maybe as decoration on a funky T-shirt he would wear to the coffee shop, one that would complement his fuzzy orange beanie. I said, "You sure use the word 'looming' a lot."

He said it was hard to get people to read a novel.

Huh?

Mike was in quicksand.

In order to deal with the fear of the unknown that accompanies us every time we take on a new activity, we often suit up. We muscle up a new self: Serious Writer Man. It's really fake.

And it *always* produces weak writing—writing that tries to please some bizarre-o notion of Posterity.

When we try to sound like Serious Writers, we usually sound like goofy kids. Trying too hard.

It's likely you will, at some point, pass through this gawky phase on your way from daily writing to book writing. It's a common pitfall.

Approach this fake-trying-too-hard self gently. This self is terrified of being superficial, of being wrong, of not being taken seriously. This self is a bit in love with the sound of its own voice and can be very convincing. It can talk you into believing everyone else—your teacher, your loyal group mates—is stupid and that it alone is for real.

Serious Writer Man needs something to do. However, write your book is *not* it.

You can let Serious Writer Man write *about* your book. But he can't be allowed in your writing room where *you* are creating the real thing.

Your book has to sound like you.

The bigger your project, the plainer your voice.

The bigger your dreams, the more grounded your book's reality.

You have to learn to get over yourself. And if the self is very high up, that can be hard to do. You'll have to jump high or deflate the obstacle.

One of my teachers solves the Serious Writer Man problem by always working on two novels at once. The real novel and the decoy novel. She has both notebooks—she always writes by hand—out on her desk. When she gets a whiff of Serious Writer Man (he wears way too much patchouli) coming down the pike, she switches from her Real Novel notebook to the Great American Novel notebook and lets him have his say.

Serious Writer Man is the guy you avoid at cocktail parties. He knows a lot. You feel you *should* like him, *should* listen. But really you want to be over in the corner, with the teenagers in jeans who are describing everyone else at the party with perfect vision. You'd rather be with your friends.

It was really hard for Mike to give up the Great American Novel. He wasn't entirely sure it was a good idea to not sound important. *Books sound important. All his favorite books had the word "looming" in them. What was wrong with "looming"?* He didn't quite trust me.

I knew Mike had to be lured back to book writing—back to his real book, not this fake shimmery flashy thing—by doing what he did best, in a straight line, for a long time. We laid out his favorite pieces on my office floor, the greatest hits from his pre-Serious Writer Man phase.

We found ways to expand two of the pieces—the Grim Reaper and His Roommate was so great, it could really be four pieces. And the Sticker Girl piece could be made into a series. By working with the best parts of the Reaper piece and the Sticker material, he thought he could also insert a third narrative line: vignettes from his musician friends' world, which would work as little commercial breaks or word-photographs between the other stories.

Mike wrote this book.

When he looks back, he says, reddening, "Who on earth did I think I was?"

Serious Writer Man is *very* convincing. The minute you start living out your book dream, he's going to try to help you.

Mike's mistake was a voice slippage: adopting a false or lofty attitude that *seems* really smart and right and yours. But it's not. It's so easy to lose your voice when you want to write a book very badly. You want to impress the world. It's a lot like buying a stiff navy blue suit for a job interview. It *seems* like what people wear to interviews. We all do this—we adopt the trappings of a new role, trying to get comfortable in it but looking faintly ridiculous. Mike's a beanie/Converse/rust-colored cords kind of guy, and his Great American Novel was as wrong on him as pinstripes and a wide red tie.

Mike's mistake happens to almost every writer at some point. Our heads get turned. We feel like we need to step up to the plate and write a serious book (or a humorous book, or a great book, or a New Age book, or a series). When we're driven to please, to fit in, to "try hard," we're prone to producing work that rings hollow. But it's so hard to see.

When you look in the mirror, when you read your book out loud, it seems grand and impressive and original.

We all go through this awkward phase of forcing our work into a desirable and serious suit. Seriously uncomfortable. All wrong.

It takes time and practice to trust your own voice, your own taste—to trust that your greatness will shine through. Henry David Thoreau said, "Beware of all enterprises that require a new set of clothes." Apply this maxim to your writing life. If you can't write in your normal speaking voice, about your normal daily life, wearing your regular jeans and T-shirt and no-name white sneakers, *be careful.* You might be in the midst of a mistake.

It's not easy to let go of that not-you voice—it's as convincing as Wall Street clothes are intimidating—but you have to in order to uncover your real power and true energy. Take off the suit. Get naked (see chapter 23). Trust the comfy clothes you reach for day after day, your plain, regular essential self.

ON YOUR PAGE: *Exercise 9*

Read your work out loud regularly and assess the fit. This "comfort check" exercise will help you spot your own Serious Writer Man slips. Sit alone in a quiet room and read your work out loud in order to check the quality of its tone. Some writers read into a tape recorder and play back their work; I have found that activity to be extraordinarily helpful. Listen for the extra adjectives, the show-off passages, the false notes where you are simply trying too hard.

Listen from the very center of yourself. Pare down to the essential you—not writer you, not famous you, not super you, not wretched you, just pure you. As you listen, focus on the tone of voice you hear. Ask yourself, *Is this writing most exactly me, my truest self? Am I revealing a little more than I want to reveal or am I all covered up?* As you listen try to get a visual: *If this writing were dressed, what would it be wearing?*

Read your work out loud regularly in order to determine if you're sending your writing off in a stiff, formal first-day-of-school package or in an ill-fitting tux to an event where everyone else is going to be wearing khakis.

After each read-aloud session, try revising your work. Can you do a revision that reads ultra-comfortable, natural, I-own-this-playground-in-my-denim-duds?

Stay true to your voice. Your voice is perfect in its natural, unfettered, undressed-up state.

Chapter 10
The Burden of Being (Everything to Everyone)

MOST WOULD-BE BOOK WRITERS SAY THEY CAN'T FINISH their book projects because they don't have enough time. This might be a case of misdiagnosis. A possibly fatal misdiagnosis.

Yes, often it *looks* like time (that is, the absence of) is the culprit.

However, most successful published authors (a) have other jobs in addition to book writing, (b) families, (c) everyday life challenges, and (d) sleep requirements. And all book authors have exactly the same amount of time: 24-hour days, 365 of them a year.

So, it's probably *not* time that keeps books from getting completed. Not exactly.

The core issue here is energy.

You can't write if you're exhausted, distracted, "too busy," hectic, and rushing around. Those states of being *push writing out the window.* If you're drained, you probably won't be able to sustain a creative life. After all, it takes a lot of *creative energy* to engage in a conversation, deal with annoying people, make meals, please co-workers, entertain children, and tend to the very elderly.

An enormous amount of creative energy.

If you clot your life with fabulous enriching group activities—book group, writing group, Keno, walking group, play group, hospital board, guys' night out, girls' night out—not only do you not have time to write, you don't have the energy left over to concentrate on your work. You're worn out. You've been authoring *a busy life*, and there's not enough of you left over for a writing life.

More importantly, if you're involved in activities other than writing, it's likely that you're engaged elsewhere even when you're at the writing desk. Writers need to be like Zen students. We require Still Pond. That is, psychic space in which *nothing else is happening.* If you're a frantic scheduler, it's likely you're carrying around the Burden of Being Everything to Everyone.

It's a huge energy suck, this Burden of Being Everything. It can blind you to you.

And you need self-awareness and a lot of energy—run-a-marathon energy—in order to write a whole book. Even a short easy book. It will take everything you have, plus more.

You can't Be Everything all the time, giving away all your energy to people and organizations and planned group activities. You must have mental space.

It takes quite a bit of energy on your part—a real effort—to maintain that space. You have to put a wall around a part of yourself and protect it from the world of Needs and Stuff and Functions.

Writers can come across a little weird. You already know that. We are not anti-social. We are not unkind. We are simply conserving our energy. We have to.

If it helps, you can tell people while you're writing your book that you have been diagnosed with a rare disorder, something like chronic fatigue syndrome, but they don't have a name for it. I can diagnose you. I'm a doctor. And the name, which we can keep secret between us, is: I-am-writing-a-book-itis.

That's what you must have.

Earlier this semester, I asked my class how they liked a visiting writer who had been on our campus for three days. Bethany said, "A little brusque."

I cocked my head. "Really? How so?" I tried to remember a moment during the visit when I felt brushed off—I couldn't.

"Yeah, kind of distant," Corrie said. She nodded firmly.

Then I remembered.

This had happened before.

Last month, a poet was termed "harsh." A loopy, elegant woman in her fifties. I didn't find her that way *at all.*

But the students had also called her "distant."

We are used to people going out of their way to make a nice space around themselves for us to be in.

Writers can't do that all day, every day and still have enough *energy left for writing*. I hate to see the writers I work with beating themselves up for not getting their writing sessions in every day, but I can see why it happens: They use themselves up greasing the wheels of social interactions. Even if you're good at greasing wheels, it takes a lot of fuel.

You can't do both.

Making sure everyone around us is comfortable all the time is a habit many of us have. And it's a hard one to break. Writers are focused people. Famous writers don't come to campus to make each student feel seen, comfortable, blossoming, and adored. They aren't rude. They're focused. When you're actively working on a book (and these writers were), you're in training mode. You're *surrounded*. Even when you're chatting with people in the hallway, part of you is *in the book* and not there.

Save part of yourself. You must hold yourself back. *For the book*.

Practice giving a little less of yourself to Everyone and Everything (yes, you can!).

At the beginning of the school year, two of my new students, Kami and Michelle, invited me to tea in their dorm room. They were first-year students and I was excited about the tea. It's not often I am invited to a student dwelling.

When I arrived at the appointed time, the girls were very surprised.

"I forgot," Kami said. The room was so small she could open the door and stay seated at her desk. She didn't get up out of her chair.

"Oh," I said. "Well, hello." I tried to be very nice, extra nice. It was clear she was depressed.

"I can make tea," Michelle said. She smiled and held up a mug with horses on it. She, too, was very nice, extra nice since they had invited me and forgotten. She wanted to *make up for it*.

"But we would have to go down three flights," Kami said. She sighed and swiveled in her desk chair. Michele pointed out where I could sit, on a chair cushion that was on top of their small fridge.

"We call it the living room," she said.

I said I wasn't really thirsty, which I wasn't, and I didn't want basement tea anyway so I was relieved. I settled onto a little cushion, bright pink, and said, "Why don't we just talk."

Michelle put the mug on Kami's desk, and Kami put her markers back in it. When the girls stopped trying to be so nice, stopped feeling bad about forgetting they invited me, things opened up. Our energy was freed up; we weren't *trying to do this draining thing of being polite, helpful, mannered, cordial. Everything.*

The girls showed me their photos, collages of sisters and boyfriends and brothers and parents and proms. We talked about their classes and their trips home, about what they would be for Halloween, and about how fun it was to hang around little kids. They also said how it was hard to be so nice to everyone in the cluster—fourteen girls total—and how some were very annoying. But still, you had to be friendly. All the time.

"And then there's procrastination." Kami put her head on the desk. "Like right now," she said, all muffled and weird because her face was on her notebook.

"We're terrible procrastinators," Michelle said, grimacing and nodding, a true confession. Like they were somehow aberrant, and also wicked. "We spend a lot of time not doing anything, but trying to get started on something. That is probably the thing that takes up the most time."

The tea party forced me to connect two important writing-life insights. We spend so much of our time Being Everything to Everyone, why on earth are we surprised when we have nothing left but the swamp of procrastination to stew in? The girls aren't procrastinating. They're exhausted from Being Everything all the time. If our day—our very path to the writing desk—is studded with opportunities to Be Everything, how do we expect to have energy to focus on our work, our imaginative work, this fragile challenge, this book-writing endeavor, which demands *everything we have to give*?

Can't do it. It just doesn't work that way.

There is a more straightforward approach. It requires radical self-honesty, a thing you're entirely capable of. It requires you to develop confidence and a slightly thicker skin. It asks you to walk through the lined-up couches of roommates and past the desks of co-workers, *polite and appropriate but not creatively interacting.*

You can't do this little dance for everyone, make each conversation sparkling and fun for both of you. You have to be more regal. More distant. Save the buzz for the book.

I do not attend senior dinner. I do not have lunches out with friends (I read that Maya Angelou doesn't have lunches so I stole that from her life). I do not have e-mail at home (I would get nothing done), and I do not have cable so I am unable to discuss programs with people at functions. I wait at least twenty-four hours before agreeing to do anything. I do not answer my phone when I am working.

"You could get caller ID, and then see who it is!" my friend Pamela said to me. So that if I saw it was her I could pick up. But I can't pick up, not for anyone, not when I am working.

I just smile and nod and look confused and mutter something about technology and cost and government spying and vision problems.

No caller ID.

No, no, no. That wouldn't be nice *for my book.*

I do not feel guilty about my writing time.

Not ever.

I do not feel badly about not answering the door or phone or e-mail when I am working. I am simply not available when I am working, just like anyone! A doctor doesn't take calls when he is prepping a foot for bunion surgery. He can't have lunch if the surgery takes longer than expected. He just isn't available. He keeps his energy for the task at hand. As you must be nicest first to your book.

When I invite the muse over for tea, the kettle is hot and ready. The mugs are washed and in place. I focus everything on her. And then I am available for whatever is next.

You do not have to stop Being Everything, but you have to protect your energy reserves by not giving Everything over to Everyone all the time. Hold back. Save good energy for yourself. This is not rude. In fact, most people will not even notice. It's wisdom.

Save yourself.

ON YOUR PAGE: *Exercise 10*

What drains your energy? What forces you to the reserve tank? Make a list of everything you do in a week—laundry, social engagements, neighborhood stuff, family commitments, sports, reading. Which events—even if they are intense or taxing in some way—leave you energized, fed? Which make you feel antsy, needy, bored, or just slightly frustrated? Which have "shoulds" attached to them? Which do you engage in freely, not because anyone is "watching" or "expecting" it of you?

Circle the activities or people or situations that drain you more than they feed you. Make a radical scary promise to *stay away* from those activities. You're writing a book. You can't do such a difficult thing on an empty tank.

Make a second list of activities that take up creative parts of you. Talking with your girlfriends at lunch. Jogging through the dunes with Charlie, your spaniel. Working at the soup kitchen. Teaching. It is likely going to be hard to give up these activities because they are so fulfilling, they are feeding the creative you. Look at the list honestly. Is there enough of your creative energy left over for a book? Do the math.

Chapter 11

Once Upon a Whine

Last weekend, I was at a conference in Lansing. At the opening cocktail party, a man asked me what I was working on, and I told him a memoir about face blindness. If I were him, I would have asked, "What the heck is face blindness? Are you kidding me?"

But he said, "What do you hear back from agents, anything constructive? I sent my novel off last year, and the guy writes me back and says the plot is a little soft. What the hell does that mean?"

He lifted his plastic glass, swayed, and stared at me intently. (I got the strong feeling he had had a few drinks before the party—which was dry.)

I attend almost a dozen writing conferences each year, sometimes as a participant, sometimes as a presenter, and there is always an awful lot of whining. We all do it. It's hard not to do it. But the whining thing needs to be addressed so we can take responsibility for our part in it and get on with writing our book.

That man from the conference, anyone walking down the street—a kid even—could have told him what that letter meant. It meant: Don't be an idiot. It meant: You haven't finished polishing your book. It meant: You haven't made it as great as you can make it, because you are scared to plunge in and do nothing except this book until it's done, really done. It meant: You are holding back. It meant: You haven't sent it to enough places.

This guy, I hate to say, was totally stuck in that old high school fantasy that gets all of us sometimes: Famous Writer Fantasy. And he isn't even enjoying it! He *wants* to be a writer. But he doesn't *want* to do all the work necessary to actually become a writer and publish a book. He is stuck in the sweet, sad-sack state of *wanting to be.*

He's done more than many have done—he's completed a manuscript and sent it out. To one place. But he really hasn't started. At the conference, he occupied a position above the other people who were standing in our little cluster in a nook in the dining room.

"It seems like you haven't gotten serious yet," I said to this guy. I would never see him again. There was a full moon. As I spoke, I checked to see if I would regret being so direct. No, I was calm. I was happy. My tone was inviting and helpful and encouraging. My words were true.

He reeled back.

Phil, the tall, strong, elderly man in a nice suit next to me said, "She is right. You haven't even started until you have queried fifty agents." Phil had published two books. He explained them to us in brief, sparkling paragraphs.

The man said, "Yeah, but you change it based on what they want, and then you find out they're out of business! Or they tell you something else is wrong with it. You could spend your whole life chasing your tail."

Phil excused himself saying he didn't want to monopolize my time. *Good line,* I thought.

The man said, "Do editors even *know* what they want?"

I followed Phil. A man who didn't whine, didn't listen to whining, and had, after the age of sixty-five, published two books.

Here is a list of the other comments I heard at that conference—just in one day at lunch in the buffet line when we were all harvesting our cold cuts to make our sandwiches.

- I never can finish.
- I can't tell the good stories because my daughter would die if she found out.
- I can't write now, I have a family.
- I hear so much conflicting advice.
- I live in the sticks.
- I have to wait until certain people are dead in order to write what I want.
- Grammar is so bad these days. It makes me sick.
- All the publishers are owned by one company now.
- You can't break in.
- Editors don't even read things. I know.
- Do any of us really have a chance?
- Could you believe that woman in the 9 A.M. session who sang?
- Editors don't even read the stuff they receive!
- I just don't have any confidence.

I was listening and being friendly, sliding mustard on my bread and wondering, *What's up with the whining? Why do we talk like this?* I have participated heartily in my own share of it:

- My colleagues don't appreciate my work because it isn't "scholarly."
- I can't take criticism. Just tell me what you like.
- People read my book and say they don't like it, but they aren't even my target audience.
- This is so much more work than it is worth! Why am I doing it?
- I'm exhausted.
- I'm so sick of this book.
- I'm out of ideas.
- Everyone in my department got a party when they published except me.
- I've just gone through a divorce.
- My parents are both sick with Alzheimer's; this is a bad year.
- Everyone is critical. Why do people say things that are so mean?

It's really just whining. We're a bunch of kids! Whining.

During the writing of this book, I realized I had gone down a wrong path at great speed (see Chapter 5: Slow Is Fearless). Terrified I had nothing more to say and stunned I had agreed to write *another book on writing*, I found myself coming to a pleasantly screeching halt in that lunch line.

I was whining. Not learning. Not paying attention. A little kid from the back seat of my psyche had sprung loose from his car seat and he was driving my car! Very poorly! He couldn't see out the windshield, and I was letting him call the shots! *This writing business just gets you criticized, and it doesn't pay, and no one understands.* Then, he'd laugh his sick little whiny baby laugh, and I, crying, *allowed him to do this!*

The conference attendees were robbing themselves of learning. They were bonding, like humans do when gathered around an animal corpse on which we are hungrily feeding. *I'm not getting my share. I need more attention. I don't really wanna do it. I'll do it but only if you promise you will love it.*

Whine, whine, whine!

That day, in Lansing, at 12:07 P.M., I looked at my watch.

I stepped out of line.

I put my tray down. I walked down the stairs and into the bathroom, and I washed my hands. In a kind of OCD way. It was a *ritual cleansing.*

I was going to stop whining.

It is not easy to do. To our ears, our whines sound like insights, fair complaints, justice, celebrations of the common human plight, very real problems, bonding material (things that connect us to others), good corrections for other people's bad thinking.

It's hard for us to hear our whines because we're usually feeling nervous and afraid *but we do not let ourselves acknowledge the fear.*

As you talk to others about writing, try to have your Fair Listener up and running. This is superbly hard to do, but you aren't a beginning writer, and you aren't that young anymore.

Looking back, are there times when you whined about writing but you really thought you were completely justified? It's often the tone that tips me off to my whining and I find tone by listening to my *body*. When I am whining, my voice is a bit louder than normal, and I sound very serious, verging on insistent (because in my heart, I know I'm full of bullshit so I strain to sound really convincing to myself). What about your body? When you whine, is your jaw tight? Your voice deeper? Do you tap the table, pull on someone else's arm to bring them down into the quicksand with you? Is there a righteousness involved?

You aren't at your best when you're whining, but your brain will tell you that you are the rightest little dude in the room. At this point, if you can just hear other whiners and keep track of what constitutes Fear in a Whine Suit, you'll be halfway home to seeing your own.

ON YOUR PAGE: *Exercise 11*

When you get into a whine phase, seduce your book project back into the light by getting cocky, sexy, a tiny bit inappropriate, a little bit out there. Fake pure unadulterated confidence. You get better at flirting with practice. Make a fool of yourself. Nothing bad happens. (In whining, bad things do happen! You lose friends, you attract negative people, and you are blocked from taking in positive information. Plus you are driving without a license—who put you in charge?)

What's the cockiest thing you could do for your book right now? Pull the car over. Surprise everyone. What's the grand gesture, the wild thing? Infuse the relationship with an amazing shot of passion. Freak your book out a little. Make a list of incredibly confident things to say about the book-in-progress. Make a list of intrusive but useful questions to ask other writers. Introduce a destabilizing element. Don't worry about rejection—flirting is always *play*. You aren't *serious*.

Chapter 12
Layers of Should

THERE ARE LAYERS OF SHOULD IN WRITING A BOOK.

I should *have started sooner. This* should *sound better. I* should *have more education. I* should *be done by now. I* should *be more literary. I* should *be more plot driven. I* should *like writing this book more. People* should *love this book. I* should *not sound so small town. I should write about this topic. I* should *not write about that one.*

Shoulds bind and strangle your work, they limit it, and they make your writing hours much more difficult and anxiety ridden than they need to be. Worse, they infect the writing itself—your choice of topic becomes a should, your tone becomes driven by a should, the structure of the book is informed by a should.

What's a should? A "reason" your ego uses in order to try to whip you into shape, writer-shape. But they never work. The ego *never* has good ideas for writers. Shoulds almost always send writers down the wrong path. The ego is scared of losing its job. It has to exist. Writing, however, is driven by the unconscious mind, a part of self the ego has no control over. That freaks it out. Writers steer by *wonder and desire.*

This is the opposite of should.

On the first day of a class or workshop, I always ask my students what they want to write and why.

"I have to write about my family because no one is going to believe how wacky we are."

"I wish I could write about my love for sewing. But it's so boring. So I'm working on a cookbook. You can make a lot of money with those."

"I am writing about my faith in God."

"My idea was stolen. I want to know about copyright."

"My life's project is genealogy but right now I am writing this detective thing. We're traced back to 1500s Ireland."

"I'm an experimentalist."

"I love fantasy fiction, especially erotic fantasy."

"I have to write a bestseller—I'm going to have to support myself with my writing. I can't just goof around for years on end."

"I want to write the Great American Novel."

"I want to help children, so I am writing young adult novels with uplifting messages."

A should-fest. Can you spot the shoulds in the above reasons, all of which sound like perfectly lovely reasons for writing? The shoulds layer over these writers' dreams, and every single one of the projects mentioned above is going to be *hard writing.*

Beware.

There's another kind of writer, though—there's always at least one in every class. On the first day when I ask her what she wants to write, this kind of writer says, with a kind of strange half-smile on her face, "I do not know. I'm not quite sure. Maybe I'm here to find out?"

There's always a quiet in the room. A collective sigh. A focusing. This writer is brave. And she is the one writer who, should-free, will get to her true material, her most natural voice, and the correct shape for her book fastest, easiest.

I want to find out is your anti-should; steer by it.

Without a should, you are free-floating. Yes! Writers are people who are training themselves to be comfortable not knowing.

A should is like water wings, a false sense of security. You are floaty with a should, puffed up, inflated. You won't sink. But you won't swim, either. With a handy should, you've got your little mission statement, you're a fine little company, you have a raison d'etre.

With an open *I-want-to-find-out* attitude in place of a should, you have the freedom that accompanies uncertainty. You are working hard, moving forward, swimming without the aid of should-wings. No, you can't see the shore, you can't lay eyes on exactly where you are going, where you will end up. You are *in* the book. Not outside of it, driving it. You have to be in that deep in order to write, you really truly do.

Know that it is normal to crave a should for protection, for security. Know that anyone swimming across a giant lake alone (very much like what it is to write a book) is teaching herself to deal with panic. She alternates between steady progress, stopping to poke her head up and look around, catch her breath. And then, so oriented, it's back to work.

"Should I be doing this?" is going to come up. Not a helpful question to ask when you are in the middle of a giant lake. Replace should ("I *should* swim across this lake/write this book so my family will be impressed") with curiosity and attention to the tiniest details. "If I cup my hands, do I go faster?" "If I write in present tense, do things flow differently?"

There are so many layers of should. People write books in order to try to please others in their lives. People write books because they want to make money and be famous. People write books in order to feel more cohesive, more valuable, more seen, more heard. There are so many levels to this should thing.

You can't write in order to get other people to love you. That happened to me as I was working on this book. A giant should enveloped me. It was like I was swimming across book-writing lake all tangled up in a clear plastic shower curtain. While writing the book, I was also going up for a promotion at my job. In academia, where I work, books without footnotes are sometimes looked upon like rowdy paint-stained kindergartners; they're kind of told to *hush.* I got this idea that *Chapter After Chapter* should have footnotes. Be really smart. Super-duper impressive to my dean. Smart with big words, charts, *an index.*

When I sent the first draft to Kelly, my editor, she sent it back and said something happened to my voice. "I know the problem," I said. (When you're motivated by a should, remember, you feel very strong, very clear about things. There's not a lot of doubt.) "I should have an index," I told Kelly. She said, "Well, that could be interesting. *Page After Page* doesn't really have that sort of feel, though. It's more personal."

But I couldn't hear her. All I could hear was that something was wrong with the book, and if I worked harder on the path I was on—*should, should, shoulding*—all would be healed. My book would be great. My promotion would sail through. My colleagues would love me and say, "We had no idea she was so bright!" My great horrifying should was this: *They should love me. They should respect my writing.*

This is a terrible reason to write a book, and that should will kidnap all your good ideas and hold them hostage. It was horrible, and hard, trying to get the should out of *Chapter* and the true book on the page. I could tell something was wrong—I kept banging against that plastic shower curtain—but I had no idea what it was; the should told me *work harder, learn more hard words, figure out how to do footnotes, research!*

And I did.

It took three drafts and fourteen months of work to figure it out.

My writing life had gotten hooked on a should. Writing to get people to like you *doesn't work.* Writing in order to get respect, money, fame, glory *doesn't work.* Maybe the world *should* love you, but you're not going to make that happen by writing a book to *insist* on some part of yourself.

I had to relearn to be in that place with *Chapter After Chapter* where I wanted to *find things out.* How does a person write a book? What stops so many great books from getting finished? Why do so many people walk around *thinking* about writing books, feeling they *should* be writing books? How did I write my other books, and what do I have to share that could be helpful to a few others? I had to recapture that gentle curious half-smile, that calm me. The girl who can tread water or float in the middle of a huge lake and not be scared, because she knows she can make it the whole way.

It was at a writing conference last year when I realized my own should action was snarling my draft and making my editor come up with really creative ways to tell me *you aren't writing your own book.* I was leading an all-day session titled "Revising Your Completed Novel Manuscript." (There are at least two shoulds lurking in that title—not my title, I was just assigned to it.)

We sat around a beautiful fireplace, clucking along happily in March on this island off of Seattle. Each person brought his or her novel-in-progress. The novels were in the laps of the students, like sleeping babies. My job was to help them design a revision strategy. I could feel a lot of tension in the beautiful room of this old cottage, and I could sense a lot of resistance. The students didn't want to revise their manuscripts. They wanted *agents. Agents to say these are brilliant books!!! DO NOT CHANGE A THING!* Should alert: When we have worked hard on our book and finished it, we *should* get it published.

I asked the students to briefly describe their projects.

When I came around to Nancy, a beautiful woman in her late sixties with thick black hair and an accent that sounded British but not the snobby flavor, just smart and kind and good, like tea, like a Rolls-Royce, she stroked the thousand-page manuscript that sat politely on her green nubby skirt. She summarized the plot, which took a long time, and at some point, after she'd referred to her son and his work for the government nine times, I asked her the question on all our minds: "Is this your book or his?"

"Oh, he wrote it," she said. "And then he got busy. It's too good not to finish it."

"So, it's not your book?"

"It is so good. He is a brilliant writer," Nancy said, sounding so certain in her clipped British accent. "I just have to see it published. I have to! This should be published!" She tapped her long slender fingers on the pile of pages.

One thousand pages.

What a great mom. I wanted to tell Nancy her support and pride in her son was gorgeous; I wanted to tell her what a great job she did, raising this fighter pilot.

But what a not-great writing idea this should book was.

I doubted Nancy would ever be able to finish this book, not because it was someone else's, but because of the many, many shoulds that were wrapped tightly around the manuscript.

You have to write your own book. The one only you can write. No one else. This takes fearlessness, but the exciting good news is *doing the book teaches you the fearlessness you need.*

My friend Ann has begun a book of nonfiction essays on aging, Vermont, and her lifelong adoration of Camus, among other things. She started it when we were in graduate school together. Several of the essays are finished, and she has outlined the remaining ones. An editor from a good university press has shown interest. It's killing me that she will not write this book.

I think Ann *should* write this book, so I finally asked her why she won't. She said she thought I could see this book in her the same way she can see projects in students—the great material they have and the skills they have to shape it, but they never, or rarely, write these projects. We think they should. We are writing teachers, and we have book-vision: *We can see the books in you, and we want them to come out!* This is our own should: *Everyone who wants to be a writer should be a writer.*

Ann likes to work on little things. She likes things she can take with her anywhere she goes. Micro-essays, poems, drawings, tiny articles. She doesn't want to marry a giant energy-sucking beast right now. "Having the concept of the big work," she says, "can either pull you forward or be so daunting you never get to it, never get the practice of keeping your hand in, the satisfaction of a good small piece sitting right in front of you."

So Ann *shouldn't* write a book to please me or the editor. And she isn't. She's pleasing herself by creating very short essays, about one a month, at her very own pace. She's should-free. Lots of people who dream of writing books actually want to "just write" like Ann does. There is nothing minimal or lesser about her way of working. You don't have to write a book to call yourself a writer. You get to write *your way.*

Ann is one of the most curious people I know. She writes in order to find out more about what she knows, what she sees, what she thinks and feels. I can't think of a more creative, fulfilling use of writing. It's a perfect writing life. Ann says that feeling like she *should* do anything poisons it for her, that that's why she's so awful at doing writing exercises. The writing she likes most springs up from its own organic roots. Should-free.

Another man I worked with said he'd waited for retirement to begin his big book, and now that he was here, ready with the perfect space of time, he didn't know if he had the energy to do the project anymore. He felt tired. A should had drained the life of the book right out of him. It's hard to swim across a big lake in water wings. Those props restrict you—they make you tired and impede your progress. For years and years he felt like he *should* wait to start writing—wait until he had the time. And when retirement came, a new giant should appeared over him and chanted: "You should write *now*! This instant! You said you would! Do it!" He had time, he had things to say, he had waited years for this "reward." But he was derailed by a thousand-pound should that had been gathering energy for years, and he found out he didn't care about the book anymore. And he was bereft. He'd missed the window of "now."

Discerning the *should* reasons from the *good* reasons takes a lifetime of practice. Here are some ways to clarify good and should:

- Do you want to use this book project as a tool for living more perceptively, finding out more about who you are, what you are capable of? (Good.)
- Do you like telling people you're working on a book because it's cool how others are a little bit in awe of writers? (Should.)
- Do you doubt you should be spending all this time writing? (That's a double-demon should—you *should* be doing something else *and* you *should* be writing this book. Be careful. The devils of doubt and distraction breed in those should-shadows.)
- Do you imagine how proud (fill in the blank) ________ will be when they see your finished book? Do you see them, hugging you, beaming? (Should.)
- Do you see yourself writing, day after day, for life? Holding your completed book, smiling, proud? (Good.)
- Do you feel like you aren't really quite sure what the heck you are doing, where you are going? (Good.)

- Do you feel like writing a book will make you seem smarter, loftier, deeper, more serious? (Should, should, should, should.)

The should reasons will never give you enough energy to finish; they're like drugs, full of false promises, energy-draining, not feeding. They are whips. They can motivate you, but only *for the short term.* And they dry up your creativity and amplify your self-doubt. You are likely setting yourself up for *not finishing* if you are relying on the crack cocaine of shoulds.

Instead, lean into the doubt. Sit with the "I'm not sure I know how to do this." Fling the water wings and swim out deeper, slowly. You can do it. Just breathe and don't panic.

Don't write someone else's book.

Write your own book.

Shoulds ruin your choice of topic, your tone, your writing dreams.

Don't write to someone else. Write from the deepest, most central, most fully formed part of your self.

Avoid a sense of prepackaged mission. Avoid writing that pushes you along, driven by an "I must ..." or an "I need to ..." Instead, write to *discover* what you have to say. Move toward new, uncharted territory.

ON YOUR PAGE: *Exercise 12*

List ten reasons why you are writing this book. Now go over them carefully. (This is great to do with other writers, who can often spot your "shoulds" faster than you can.) Which ones are coming from an external motivation, a desire to please others or conform to some standard?

("I have always wanted to be able to say I wrote a book!" is an example of a should, as is "I know I need to get this story down on paper.")

Try to see the reasons that are coming from *other people or forces*. ("I promised my grandmother I would write her story." "My wife thinks I can do this.") Chances are, you will have a mix of good reasons and should reasons. Your task is to choose the *one heart-based reason you are really going to do this*. The rest of the reasons may be *outcomes*. But they aren't why you are doing this. It's key to get clear on this.

If you are stuck, make a different list. What is it you want to find out by writing this book? Don't worry if this is hard to complete: You are on the right track if you feel numb and a little scared and unsure. Not knowing is not a comfortable place to be. Middle of the lake. It's supposed to be big.

Once you've examined your list, copy *one heart-based, curiosity-driven* reason for writing this book on an index card in your best printing. Tape the card to your computer. After a while you won't see the card anymore—try to notice that day. Move the card, just slightly, so it catches your eye again; repeat. If you are in the habit of being eaten alive by shoulds (people pleaser, straight-A person, you know the type, and you know who you are), you need to make copies of this card and place them in your wallet, inside your fridge, on your dashboard, etc. Read the real reason every day before your session. Read it during Positioning the night before. Catch the shoulds and dismiss them. You need to power through this book on clean green energy, the renewal resource that is the curious part of your heart.

Chapter 13
Good Enough

To write a book you have to have a weird maddening mix of impossibly high standards and slutty low, low, low, standards. At the same time. The whole time you are writing.

Maddening, to say the least.

For some personality types, this high-low thing, this freaky dance, comes more naturally than it does for other types. Regardless of your tendencies—toward perfectionism, toward the slapdash, toward risk taking, toward mulling—you can work with the Good Enough principle and write a better book.

Some people don't finish their books because they don't see standards as a wheel. You cycle through standards. When you're stuck or stranded or bored with your book, lower your standards. Slouch your way through it. When you're writing high and hard and strong and solid, raise your standards.

When you're totally in flow, you can write longer. Your next three sessions might be double in length. You can realize your something big, like your subplot is completely predictable and needs to come out ... but it won't feel like your book is falling apart. High standards tell you that you're making your book much better. It's a great feeling.

It's a wheel. Every writer is on it. Spinning.

Good Enough is the contemporary way of saying something your parents told you regularly: "Do the best you can."

I didn't know what this phrase meant when I was a kid. I

didn't know *how* to do the best I could. I hadn't seen too many people do it. I had no idea what it would feel like inside, or what exactly to do. I was either soaring or freaking out.

Now I know that "do the best you can" means you put honest-to-God everything you have into your book. You can't call it Good Enough until you have stretched yourself, dug deep, pushed yourself, and really truly (you know it in your gut, in your body, in your soul) given the book everything you have. You haven't pretended to be dumber, lazier, simpler, busier, faster, smarter than you are. You bring the book up from the very depths of *you.* There's nowhere to hide—you are either working from that place or you are not.

When you are giving it your best, nothing is held back. All the parts of self converge on the goal. When you give it everything, *everything*, there are still going to be flaws. And that's when you say, at the very end of the day, Good Enough.

Good Enough isn't settling. It's celebrating the truth.

Good Enough means you know when to quit. The book can't be any better—not because you're sick of working on it but because *there are great parts*.

Good Enough means you know when to keep pushing yourself. You develop, as a more advanced writer, a sense of when you're hitting false notes. Like an actor, your feelers are increasingly sensitive. *Nope, that's not quite right. That's a little forced. I didn't come from the deep center place here. It's off.* You don't fake it. You don't close your eyes and pretend the bad parts aren't there. That's what kids do when they have to revise a report or clean their rooms. They see that the bottom dresser drawer is a mess. They feel overwhelmed, and they move on. That's not Good Enough.

Artists feel comfortable staying in a place of not knowing for extended periods of time. You must figure out how to manage those chaotic, messy, *I don't know!* moments. Practice being calm within thoughts like *I have no idea! How am I supposed to know what's good and what isn't?* Trust that as you go over this manuscript again and again and again, you will develop a sense of what to work on and how to go about it. Artists figure out, through lots of daily practice and trial and error, when fear is talking (*I can't revise! This was too hard to write!*) and when the little nudges are worth pursuing, no matter how hard or time-consuming (*Go back to the beginning, look again at how you started this thing. ... Is that right?*).

You have to find this slippery equilibrium called Good Enough.

What if for your first book you decide to intentionally write a Good Enough book? It's not going to be great. It's not going to make more than five thousand dollars. (Your pay: one dollar per hour). It isn't going to become a bestseller or change the world (although you will get a ton of e-mails from people who loved your book, telling you of the insight they have come to because of you). What if you intentionally write your first book to fill the Good Enough slot? You might actually get it done this time! Every time you freeze, lower your standards. It just has to be Good Enough!

But, at the same time, you're giving it 100 percent, your all, everything you have.

When I was finishing my Ph.D., I knew I would never be able to read enough criticism and literary commentary to do a good job. I had six months to prepare for the written and oral examinations. I had a list of books my professor told me to read and a notebook where I copied good lines and tried to work out the main points and why they were important. It was hard to see how everything fit together. I sorely wished I had paid more attention in graduate school lectures. I was pretty distracted with work, my love life, and an incredibly challenging family situation.

I loved reading, but it was scary and horrible to read these books and know there was a giant test, the biggest exam of my life, creeping ever nearer. And I was so woefully underprepared, having missed vast amounts of school as a kid. But I decided to try for this credential, the Ph.D., anyway.

It takes guts to try something you will not be great at. I am *terrible* at sitting in a room of Ph.D. types talking about books (there would be three days of this oral testing after the written component), because I can't figure out their attitude toward the books—it's a weird mix of flavors I can't get my mind around. I tend to gush over what I love and then feel embarrassed, so I bring memorized quotes, like candied fruit in a cake, and stud my conversations with those, one after another. I make no sense in these situations. But, when I allowed myself to become a Good Enough Ph.D. candidate—good, not great—I enjoyed my studies a lot more.

It is counterintuitive to fling yourself into situations that make you want to run. Every cell in your body says, "Please, no, you're dying here! Get out while you're still alive!" These physiological responses—sweating, increased heart rate, dilated pupils—are very real, and you can't really tell the difference between near death and the pain from putting yourself in an uncomfortable situation: a three-day oral test on books you haven't read, a book project that you do not know how to finish.

Doing poorly and continuing to move forward is rewriting tens of thousands of years of human development. It doesn't feel right.

Good writers learn to *ignore that feeling.* Nothing bad will happen to you if you bomb your oral examinations or if you write a book that really is kind of *awful*. You will not die. You might get a different kind of job than the one you're preparing for, you might stick that Good Enough book under your bed, but nothing has really happened that is life threatening or bad.

It will feel weird, always, to do poorly and keep going.

That's the heart of Good Enough.

Once you give your daily writing sessions your complete soulful all, you can say, "I'm good and also enough is enough." With a clear heart and a clean conscience, you will know you have truly done your best. That's Good Enough.

ON YOUR PAGE: *Exercise 13*

Is there a time when you have lowered your standards and achieved a fine outcome? It might be hard to think of these, because we are programmed toward perfection and its evil handmaiden, Quitting. When have you "settled" exquisitely in order to get through the day, through a project? Reflect or freewrite on how Good Enough thinking has played a role in your life.

Then make a list. What are ten qualities that your book must have in order to be successful *for you?* And now the hard part: Which five of these can you let go?

For example, I want my memoir to be a bestseller; to help others who suffer from face blindness receive help and support; to connect me with other face-blind people; to win a great prize; to let me remove a course from my regular teaching load; to be a book that is compelling in its structure, but also elegant and risk taking and sophisticated; to tell my whole life story; and to work as individual essays *and* as one whole book. And not to be that hard to write. With a perfect focus. And jokes!

Here are the five I have to let go of to get closer to Good Enough: bestseller, prize, removing a course, whole life story, essays and whole at once.

When I did this exercise, it surprised me that it was harder to concretize and articulate my expectations for the book than it was to let things go. Left unverbalized, those expectations turn into giant roadblocks on your path to a finished book. (This exercise also works for dating, marriage, house hunting, and so on.)

Chapter 14

Faith in Writing

NOTHING STOPS A CONVERSATION FASTER THAN SOMEONE bringing up religion. "Avoid three topics," my mother used to tell me. "Money, sex, and religion." (It turns out those are the three most interesting conversational topics; don't tell my mother.)

So, it's on tip toe that I approach this sentence: Writing a book is like having faith.

I teach at a college affiliated with the Reformed Church of America (I'd never heard of it, either), and many of my students are practicing Christians. I think their ability to keep their faith during their late teens and early twenties is one reason they really understand writing. They have already spent most of their lives believing in something that they can't see, that is powerful, that requires daily attention, and that may or may not reward them financially or otherwise. Essentially, they've been training for the writing life for two decades when they come to creative writing class! These are great writing students.

If you write a book, you are going to be monk-like sequestered, but the comparison goes deeper than just the physicality the two endeavors share. "To me, faith means not worrying," wrote John Dewey. That's what I call *a fearless, focused writer*. If you write, at some point, you give yourself over to the process. You let the book write you.

Martin Luther King, Jr., said, "Faith is taking the first step even when you don't see the whole staircase." Could there be anything more like beginning a book project than *that*? And William Wordsworth said, "Faith is a passionate intuition," implying that writing and creative concentration are the same as faith.

When you set out to write a book, you're practicing the *exact same habits of mind and spirit* that the deeply devout practice.

Writing is daily. When you're a person of faith, you're always that faith, not just when you go to the mosque or synagogue or temple or church. You might behave in unfaithful ways; you will surely slip up. Aren't most religions designed to help us understand human nature better? Isn't their point to help us be a better version of ourselves? This is exactly what a daily writing life creates in you.

Like writers, people of faith focus on processes, not results. Of course you're going to miss writing days. Of course you're going to experience Creep and the temptation of other book projects. Of course you may not finish your Book 100. That's why you have writing! It always welcomes you back. (Maybe not with open arms—after all, when you abandon your writing it can take days and days to get back in the groove—but it will welcome you back nonetheless.)

There's more to this metaphor, though.

When you write, you believe in something no one else can see. You spend lots of time committed to a project for which there are no assurances, no guarantees. Being a writer subjects you to the same doubts, the same unpopularity, the same nagging questions that believers struggle with. Writing is communing with the unseen; not everyone will understand why a normal, intelligent, educated, seemingly balanced person would devote her energy to something that can't be proven: your writing success. A novel-in-progress may not exist for a long, long time. But you believe in it anyway. And, even if you forget to believe in it, even if you doubt it, it's *still there.*

A lot of books don't get born because their authors forget to keep thinking of themselves as writers even when they fall away from their book projects.

It's just like faith. You don't really *know* if there is any way to prove this or that, but the days you do it—the days you practice—are better than the days you do not do it. Perhaps you have noticed that, occasionally, amazing things happen, little miracles like when the writing takes over and pulls you along, and it's effortless.

But mostly, you take it on pure faith, trusting that this is how you should spend your time, that the world does need your work, you're meant for something more than stumbling through life—you're meant to make sense of who we are by writing things down, *by making meaning.* The whole thing is mysterious, unprovable, slippery.

I am sometimes asked, "What is the point of having more people write? Creative writing programs are burgeoning—what is going to happen to all these writers? Not many of them can be that good."

I react badly to this question. I feel like I am being asked, "Why eat healthy vegetables if we are going to die anyway?"

Do flourishing writing programs sound like the end of civilization, a harbinger of destruction? Show me a culture where the citizens are learning to craft articulate responses to the world around them—through detective novels or

Petrarchan sonnets or articles in *Dog Fancy* or experimental graphic novels—and I see a culture of growth, of aliveness, of hard work, of thought, focus, and faithfulness.

We write on faith. Not everyone in the normal day-to-day world understands an activity that calls for hours spent alone in a room, engaged in a process that may or may not produce big bucks, fame, great photos of oneself perched on a cute sofa, Oprah. We work like the faithful work: quietly, not talking a whole lot about it. Humble, because we know a lot of the good stuff we write doesn't really come from *us* but from the mere act of practicing and opening the mind and sitting there for enough days in a row.

Not everyone agrees, of course, but I believe we're here in order to bear witness. To say what we see, what we know about it, what we notice. It's a part of our rent-paying for the space we take up on the planet. We complete our lives in a small important way by *writing*.

Being a writer, like being a person of faith, can make you feel a little separate from other people. It can make you feel a tiny bit superior. But we aren't better than other people. We're just paying better attention.

Writing is believing in something larger than yourself: the value of trading our stories around. There's no proof it works. You really don't ever *know* if you're going to get published, find success, get discovered. Is it worth it, all the hours it takes to write just one good page? You don't know if people will read your book, if anything will come of it.

To write chapter after chapter, to have enough faith to complete a book, requires a level maturity, an openness and trust in this larger other thing. That's how books get written.

ON YOUR PAGE: *Exercise 14*

If doubt is driving you and you're missing writing days, if you're not writing more than you're writing or not focusing when you're supposed to be writing, think of your writing life as a kind of faith, and get in touch with your "higher power."

What gives you the strength to write this book? What fills you with doubt? Develop your own religious rituals: What will keep you on track when doubts lead you astray? What helps you keep the faith in your book-writing project? What destroys your faith? What, for you, feeds the faith you need to get this book written? Create the creeds and rituals that make your writing religion tangible.

Chapter 15

You're Ready Now

WE THINK WE DON'T KNOW ENOUGH TO START OUR BOOKS; then when we finally begin, we feel we don't know enough to finish our books. We keep thinking we need to know more.

You have to get over the believe that you are particularly in the dark. Of course you don't feel like you know enough to write a book! No one ever feels ready to write a book.

The best way to learn to write a book is to write one. You don't need another book on writing, you don't need to be younger or older, you don't need to have more time. You don't need anything else your scared brain tells you that you need. This is one time where you must *not* look before you leap. You need to leap!

Do it!

Write the book!

Screw it up horribly. No one is going to die if you write a bad book. You've got your Book 100 covered, you've embraced the Slow Movement, you've given up whining (pretty much), and you've cleared a space under your bed. A good thing is happening: You're learning to write books.

The book is your teacher. It shows you, productively, a tiny bit at a time, what to focus on learning next. Writing a book is like taking a perfect class on how to write a book.

It's hard, though, to work in the dark like this, trusting the book. An unwritten book-in-progress feels about as chaotic and crazy as an erupting volcano. *This is my teacher? Don't teachers stand in front of classrooms and spell things out clearly? They don't torture you! Isn't there supposed to be a syllabus?*

Nope. The goal of pedagogy is to take the student from where he is right now to the next tiny possible step. Your unwritten book is a genius of a teacher. It's your guru. It will wait for you to ask it smart, productive questions. When you write a new chapter, perhaps trying something completely different, and you put your whole mind and soul into it, the book-as-teacher will reward you with new insight and—like any great teacher—the key to the next room, where you will be stunned and in the dark, not knowing and lost all over again. A one-on-one, tailor-made tutorial. Just for you.

A lot of us spend our whole lives feeling like we can't do it, can't write a book until we ____________________. Many of us are waiting for someone to explain it all to us or for *something to happen* before we start.

We read magazines that tell us we need more stuff, cleaner houses, makeovers for our faces and sofas and abdominal muscles, our parenting must be different, our sex life needs to improve, and we need lots more education before we fancy ourselves writers. If I'm not careful when I walk past the covers of those magazines, I start to feel like I know nothing and am completely wrong. This is not a good place for a writer to spend too much time.

Let your book be your teacher.

You *are* ready for this.

When you write a book, you become a wonderful student again. It's humbling. You will be tested. You'll feel as though you'll never master it all (you won't). You'll often feel lost and confused, wondering *How does this all fit together? What is the point?* Trust that it's going to work out, that you *will* get it. Believe me. I know how hard it is.

I always want to know *before I start* what the heck I'm doing.

That's stenography, not writing. It's recording, not learning. Writing books doesn't work that way. Stop waiting for it to "feel right" to start. It won't. Ever.

Some teachers call it the growing edge, this part of you that is in constant contact with the unknown, the new, the about to be.

In yoga class, the handstand is a big deal, really hard, scary, dramatic. We want to do it but we quiver in fear, not feeling ready. Some people *aren't* ready—they do not have the upper-body strength, the knowledge of what their shoulders are doing, *the foundation.*

For those of us who have been taking yoga classes for years and lifting weights are completely physically prepared. Mentally, though, we struggle to get our bodies to do something they haven't done. It's fear. Our bodies don't want to be upside down. The brain says, "Me, on the bottom? Terrible idea! I do not hang from that little stalk, the neck! I rule from up top!"

You are completely ready to write your book; you have the stamina, you have the strength, you have the focus, and you have the fear. Bring that fear along with you and use it to illuminate your path.

When you do something you haven't done before—like writing a book or maintaining a handstand—your brain will send messages screaming *Abort! Abort! Abort!* There aren't neural pathways to support this new work. We humans survived by *repeating what worked last time.* However, you can't finish your book by repeating old behaviors. You have to explore new territory.

Writing a book is going to annoy the hell out of your brain. What you are asking it to do—to always move toward the unknown—goes against thousands of years of successful survival. That's a lot to be up against! But that's how we evolve. We take chances. We don't stay stuck in our tiny limitations. We fly. We go to the moon. We create symphonies. We do this by moving toward the unknown, not pulling back from it.

I am going to learn how to do this! is the most powerful motivational statement I can think of for writing a book. Not to get money or fame, not to get people to fall in love with you, not to impress your children or avenge your parents, but to learn: *I am going to learn how to do this.*

I started to pay attention to my students who wrote a lot on their own outside of class. These were the ones who improved. What was their reason for writing? It came from deep inside. It had nothing to do with me or the class. Some other force took over and kept them, butt-in-chair, at their writing desks late into the evening. They wanted to learn as much as they could from the writing project. *It was their real teacher.* Not me.

A book project, like a good teacher, gives you a reason, a focus, a motivation that keeps you from getting lost in your head, lost in pages, lost in serial restarting. A book-writing life keeps you on the road—it's the guardrail that keeps you from falling off the cliff into the flat sea of the thinking-about-writing abyss.

"I'd like to write someday," or "I have an idea for a book," or "I have five novels I want to write," are not reasons to write. This kind of thinking is like watching other people do handstands. You learn nothing from sitting on the sidelines; you simply reinforce your fear.

A clear book project is motivation. It's a great way to structure your writing time. Just as a runner makes daily runs, one after the other, preparing for the big race, we do better writing when it's *for* something. The most common question runners ask other runners is "What are you training for?" If a writer has a live book project, she has a relationship with a treasured teacher.

You have everything you need to write this book; you know what you need to know. You know how to find out things you do not know. You have enough time (same as everybody else), enough life experience, enough smarts. You are ready to write this book.

You are ready now. Your teacher is waiting.

ON YOUR PAGE: *Exercise 15*

Make a list of everything you do not know about writing your book. Small things—how to open chapters, titles. And large things—how to plot, how to structure, what it should be about, voice, tone. Make a list of specifics—*I do not know if Joey is married. I do not know if I can include the story about Cecilia. I do not know if you are allowed to write about real people, can I use Uncle Henry?* Write everything you *do not know*. Give yourself several sessions to do this; you will think of things you do not know at odd times. Write them all down.

Then choose one. Write it. In all likelihood, you won't "do it right" the first time (just as you didn't the first time you rode a bike, got on a surfboard, solved for x). Write it again. Notice what you are learning, notice how much you already know.

Part 2

The Long Haul: Strength-Building for Book Writers

Chapter 16

Wise Guides

WRITING A BOOK IS VERY MUCH LIKE GOING ON A LONG TRIP abroad. You leave the world as you know it. But you aren't plunged into a strange land alone, without a map or compass. Writers who have gone before travel with you; all you have to do is welcome them along.

Let books be your guides.

Choose wisely.

And, most importantly, limit yourself to exactly six books per writing project.

Three books on craft. And three books *exactly like the one you wish to write.*

After you choose your Six Wise Guides, no more new writing books. Not one.

Remember: *You are a book writer; not a book buyer. You are a book reader; not a book skimmer.* To really know a book—how it's built, its wisdom—is to read it several times. To go over and over certain passages.

Many of us mistakenly give way to distraction and continually troll new writing books, looking for answers, inspiration, comfort. We get stuck or bored or cranky, and we buy a new book on writing. I should know. I get cranky a lot: I currently have on my shelves 163 books on writing. This is way too many. Do not do this. I went wide when I should have gone deep. I kept looking for the "answer"—the magic—

in outside sources when it's really in the process of working over my own book.

Some of my 163 books—the best ones—I know extremely well because I study them, teach from them, turn to them all the time (I have listed these in the appendix). Many of these 163 books were fun, helpful, inspiring, and enjoyable. Necessary? No. Could I tell you what they are about? Not really. Writing books are like chocolates. So much taste fabulously packed into such a great little package. But is chocolate necessary? No. Will it help you thrive and grow? Not so much. Do you *need* it? No. Writing books—be careful. Use them wisely.

Reading a book on writing can make you feel like you're being really creative. But, you're really only pleasantly sated, no further along on your book-writing journey than you were before. It's dangerous to think you have *done* something when, in fact, you may have only increased the feeling that you don't know enough and never will.

Dear friend, it's time to pack for the trip—the journey that is writing *your* book. You must pack light. Six is the magic number.

How do you choose your six? Beginners often pay attention to what's hot, what's new on the shelf. On the other hand, the serious book writers—the successful book *finishers*—constantly turn back to the best books on craft and the best books *like the one they want to write* (the gems of their Book 100). Choose wisely; give yourself some time here. You're going on an important voyage.

When I drafted my first novel, I read constantly. Each novel I read seemed to brilliantly solve a problem I was having, and I constantly changed direction. My draft never did come out right, nor did the one after that. I didn't know the Six Wise Guides rule. I thought I could learn from *everything.* (This is why it's best to do the bulk of your Book 100 *before* you start writing.) I wasn't learning from my reading—I was fueling my self-doubt and chasing after Sexy Next Book ideas. In short, I was getting nowhere.

I am working on a memoir this year, and I know so much more. My book is about the psychology and neurobiology of face recognition, about memory and family, about marriage and divorce, and about the role childhood plays in it all. There's science, research, memoir, storytelling, and chapters. It's a big project. But I have strictly limited myself to consulting six books as I work. No more. No less.

I have on my desk three books like the one I want to write (*A Natural History of the Senses* by Diane Ackerman, *The Year of Magical Thinking* by Joan Didion, and *This Boy's Life* by Tobias Wolff). I study how writing works not by reading *about* it but by reading *it*. I type sample paragraphs from my three models when I'm stuck. I take apart their chapters and outline them, noticing how emotion is presented, noticing what happens off the page, between the lines. I am *working* these books.

In the three books like the one *you* want to write, you will find the answers to all writing problems. When you are stuck, open one of these guides. How did the author solve the problem of how to end chapters? Read all the chapter endings in your sample books. Teach yourself how to end chapters. When you are stuck on something like plotting or dialogue, consult your guides. The three of them will put their heads together and give you answers. Every single time.

You can't plagiarize a *method* of opening a chapter. You can't really steal a technique—the techniques belong to all of us. If you love the way one of your Wise Guides does dialogue, use her patterns and cadences and beats in your own dialogue. It's not cheating. It's how all writers work. It's called *reading like a writer*.

For your second set of guides, choose three craft books.

This means that instead of constantly looking for more writing instruction (you will learn more by *writing your book*, not reading every book you can find on writing), you settle on three great ones. And then keep turning back. This is how great students study—they go over the material. Over it and over it and over it. Until they *own* it.

To learn the secrets of craft, pick from the classics, the best books on craft that have stood the test of time. Janet Burroway, Mary Oliver, William Stafford, Carol Bly, Stephen Koch, John Steinbeck. You pick.

For my memoir, I chose Robert McKee's *Story,* about how to compile story parts to make a compelling tale; John Gardner's *On Becoming a Novelist*; and Eric Maisel's *Fearless Creating.* Two structure books, and one on getting unstuck and keeping up confidence. When I feel I've reached a limit of my writing ability (this happens several times a day), I turn to one of those three. I am not allowed to look at any of my other 163 books on how to write.

The point of the Six Wise Guides is *focus*. Where something like the Book 100 gives you breadth and exposure, these select Wise Guides give you precision and exactitude. So many writers on the verge of a breakthrough get scared or nervous, so caught up in all they do not know that they wander off down a new trail, even when the wisdom, the breakthrough they long for, lies down the path they are already on … if they could just hang on a little longer, trust the process a little more.

You must severely limit your distractions during your book-writing efforts, and new books are a great distraction, one we're especially likely to entertain when the going gets tough and we're eager for a quick getaway. You can't be a wide reader while you're writing your book. Sure, you may have used the Book 100 as a ramp *into* your writing, but once you're there the training wheels have to come off. It's just too hard to be a recreational reader *and* a writer at the same time. When you are done with your first full draft, you can go on a reading vacation and catch up on all the books you missed while you were away.

At this point in your life as a writer, it's time to *deepen*. No more New Programs, no more Perfect Book Plan books. Make your choices, commit to them, and stay the course. Down. Deep. In.

A helpful warning: If there is a should sentence cropping up here, and this is very common—"I *should* really rely on Boswell's *Life of Johnson*." "I *should* really have Shakespeare on the desk." "I *should* read …"—stop. Go back to your list. What book, really, do you want to write? Should books will not sustain your book-writing project. They will suck energy from it, and you do not have extra energy when you are doing a book marathon. You can read your should books much later. Or never.

In a *Paris Review* interview, William Kennedy talked about finding his way to *his* effective problem-solving books during the writing of his novel *Legs,* which went through six major incarnations before it "clicked":

> I was thinking I would write it as a film-in-process, because the gangster had been such a charismatic presence in movies. That became a silly gimmick. I tried to make it a surrealistic novel. I tried to pattern it totally on *The Tibetan Book of the Dead*. I tried to write it from inside Diamond and it didn't work and I tired to write from outside Diamond with a chorus of voices and it didn't work. And then I discovered if I used the lawyer who was in the book from the beginning as this intelligent presence who could look at Diamond and intersect with him at every level of his life, then I would be able to have a perspective on what was going on inside the man. So I did. Five years' worth of paper at that time but three months' worth of work made all the difference. Then the book began to define itself. That's when you really understand the craft.

By trying on different approaches from other writers, Kennedy found his match and entered the world of craft, where he could finally work on his book.

The Six Wise Guides are my pit crew. I focus my writing time like a race car driver doing laps around the track, grooving down tight, and when I get stuck, blow a tire, get off track, the six books in the pit are there for me. They're watching me the whole time. They run across the pavement with their tools. They want me to succeed. They want me back in the race.

Let the six books make a tight circle around you. Consult no one else. Hire smart at the outset.

Stay with your six.

ON YOUR PAGE: *Exercise 16*

Select your six books. You are going to be highlighting, marking, annotating, Post-It-ing these books. They're like cookbooks—they're going to have food stains, sweat stains, and ink stains on them. I'm on my second copy of Robert J. Ray's *The Weekend Novelist* and my fourth copy of Janet Burroway's *Writing Fiction*. Arrange them in a good space on your writing desk. A little altar. Each day, as part of your writing time, open a couple of the books and consult the pit crew members—let them know you will be relying on them! Peruse a table of contents. Count chapters. Read one of your books for a few minutes to get warmed up. The pit crew offers you problem solving, cheerleading, wisdom, pleasure.

Prerequisite: The Book 100. If you try to assemble a pit crew without interviewing the requisite number of candidates, you are likely to make choices based on *should* reads and other unfortunate motivations. Do your Book 100 first. If you don't have time to read one hundred books, when is it you are going to find the time to write? Do your reading. Then transition that reading time right over onto your writing-time calendar.

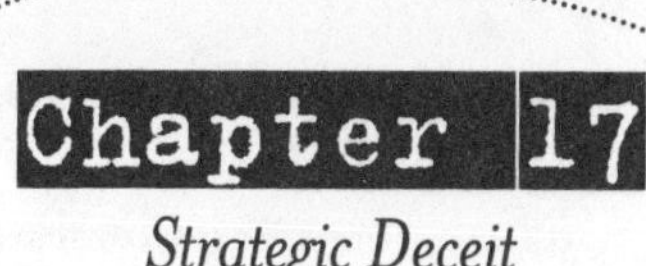

Chapter 17
Strategic Deceit

I BELIEVE THAT IF YOU ARE GOING TO FINISH A BOOK, YOU have to elevate writing to the status of family member. Your writing life, your book, really is an addition to your family. Writing has its own needs and activities and moods and stresses and joys. It clamors for your attention. It has a mind of its own.

I have learned to "shape the truth" in order to keep to my daily writing habit. Sometimes, for me, it's the only way to make sure that my writing doesn't get shoved aside. Your job as a writer is to figure out what in your community and in your own heart parts seas. What is always excused?

Elevate your writing-life commitment to that level of importance. No one else is going to do it for you.

I call what I do Strategic Deceit.

I first used it with Rick, my former boyfriend, who was incapable of leaving the house on time to make a movie, a flight, or anything whatsoever. Building time around Rick was necessary, a little Strategic Deceit. If the movie started at 2:05 P.M., I told him it started at 1:45 P.M. We would then leave the house "late," him rushing about crazed, at 1:41 P.M., and we'd arrive at 2 P.M. or so, just in time. Once Strategic Deceit was in place, we were both more relaxed. For Rick to make the movie on time, he needed *more time than other people;* I simply adapted reality to his version. Is that dishonest? Effective? Both? (After a while he caught on, and we just got a VCR.)

When lying equates to presenting a version of reality that enables a seriously productive writing session to occur, I believe we are helping ourselves and those around us sky-rocket past petty blocks and into the productive writing space.

I know this is controversial. But for me, it's necessary. I started my Strategic Deceit, Writing Version to protect my writing. I started telling friends and family I had to do Officially Blessed Activities. For a while, I was in a fake genealogy group. Amazing! No one ever questioned it or complained if I was unavailable because I had genealogy. Genealogy was my way of labeling my novel. And I do not feel remotely guilty about presenting it as a group, a decoy to get guilt off my back and give me the time I need to work. My novel is about family and generations—I feel absolutely confident of the deeper truth of my statement.

Once, I couldn't meet a girlfriend for lunch because I was working on a poem and she said, "That must be nice. Sitting around, whipping out a poem." (*Yeah, that's what writing poetry is like! Oh man.*) When I would say that I had a poetry group meeting, I got total respect from my friends and family. If I said, "I'm writing sonnets tonight, alone, in my room, not answering the phone," I got The Look.

I know lying might not be your thing. But look carefully at these familiar reasons for not writing:

- The market is too difficult.
- I never enough time.
- I just keep getting stuck.

- I'll just get rejected again.
- I can't concentrate long enough to finish.

I think there's an element of deceit in every single one of those sentences.

The reason I switched over to Strategic Deceit had more to do with honesty than lying. Having the support of my friends and family is crucially important to me—it's a big part of my writing process. When I feel I am letting people down, I get depressed and cranky, and I can't work. I blame them/me/them/me in a whole little head-eats-tail whirlwind of blame and neurosis.

If I can honestly get to my writing sessions every day, and *keep the promise I made to myself no matter what—to work on this book every single day, eyes open, heart open*—I am living the best life I can live. I keep my promises to other people, I sleep better, and I can honestly, openly say, with pride, "I am a writer."

Sitting alone in a room and concentrating hard and wisely and well on your book is *fragile.* It's not like sitting through a meeting or washing dishes. It's a fragile state that is easily broken open—there are a thousand distractions, internal, external. Writing demands a very precise state of mind, and it's not easy to get into (the daily habit is the only thing that makes writing a little bit easier).

So I don't mind having to lie to buy my way into that space. I think the lie also protects me. When everyone else knows what I am doing—*Oh, she is in there writing!*—it can feel a bit pressured, like I better produce great stuff. It can feel like I am typing under a floodlight, with the world watching. That's a great way to ensure constant distraction.

Strategic Deceit is polite. It lets me slip out, unseen,

into the pocket of space and time where art is made. No big drama—*Oh, she is writing now! Don't make a sound!*—I'm just leaving the meeting quietly to go do my work.

Weird?

Well, probably so. *Writers are not like other people.* It's a lie to try to pretend we are. We have to steal the time for our work from somewhere.

ON YOUR PAGE: *Exercise 17*

Make a list of ten Strategic Deceits you could use to counter everyday demands and obligations (stay late, make dinner, haul someone somewhere, join a new committee, take on extra work for an old one, etc.). Use things that have gotten you "free space" in the past. For example, if you say, with a really serious, slightly fragile look on your face, "This is a particularly difficult time for me," you can get out of some things that you really should not be participating in. And, it's true! The best lies, as we all know, are honest.

If you are writing a book about World War II, what could you say you are doing that would buy you time? Helping a group of vets recapture their memories? Which you are, see? Your book will help so many people! If you are writing a novel about nuns in the seventeenth century, you can *easily* come up with ways to present that one. Hint: Focus on the nuns, not the act of *book writing*.

For some, this whole Strategic Deceit thing will just sound hideous and wrong. For you, there are other ways to get your hours in, your daily writing. And, it would be helpful if you shared what works with the rest of us. Meanwhile, you can *try* a Creative Label ("Daddy's going to sit zazen now," or "I'm training for my triathlon now, see you in two hours!"). Just to see, once, how it feels. You don't have to do it again.

Chapter 18

Staying in Love With Your Book

I WAS SINGLE AND IN MY EARLY THIRTIES, AND I WANTED TO get married. So I went to a therapist to get insight on how one might go about such a project. The therapist, a kindly older man, gave me homework in the first session.

"Make a list of everything you are looking for."

I like homework, always have. I love lists. They make messy things into a straight line. This reminded me of something I would have done with my girlfriend Sara in fifth grade. But it felt awkward and humiliating to be doing it at age thirty-one. Alone.

I came back the next week with my homework assignment completed. A twenty-nine item list that began:

1. Kind
2. Funny
3. Smart
4. Hard working
5. Creative, energetic
6. Adventurous
7. Calm
8. Crazy about me

Embarrassed and giggly, I read him the list. And when I finished he said, "Long list."

"I don't know ..." I started but he interrupted.

"When you are all those things, then you'll attract that guy. Meanwhile, work on becoming those things yourself."

At first, my feelings were hurt.

Later in the week, I decided the therapist was crazy. (He was, a little.)

Then, unfortunately, I interpreted his words to mean "set your sights lower."

Work on myself?

I wanted to get married.

Does any of this sound familiar? (*Work on myself? I just want to write a damn book.*) The whole thing—the list, the expectations, the sights-too-high/sights-too-low pitch and roll action—is how many of us continue to relate to our writing projects. Many would-be authors maintain a similar impossible quest type of relationship with their book. I know writers who are not starting their books because they want to write *the perfect book.* Their list of "how it must be" is amazingly long. They can't imagine any imperfections in this book-that-doesn't-exist.

"My magnum opus," Brandon calls his. He refuses to start writing because he doesn't think he is ready; he'll wreck it if he tries now. So he thinks about writing, talks about writing, takes writing classes, but never lets himself write the thing he feels he was put on this planet to write. His list of things to describe the perfect book he will write is so long—his rose, turning to ash as he readies and readies and readies himself for this perfection.

It's like that long list of mine that essentially described no one on the planet; it was just a list of the good qualities humans are potentially capable of (and probably not all at once).

If you want to write the perfect book, think about whether you can be the perfect *person* for it. My therapist was right. Making a list of the Great Things People Can Be and looking for a man who was all of those things was a pipe dream. I needed to see myself as an evolving, growing person. The list was just a blocking strategy, one designed to keep me very, very alone.

Your book's going to have many flaws—just like you. And me. Good intentions and bad habits, brilliant days and sucky weeks, all swirled together. Isn't it your flaws that make you *interesting and complicated?* If you are waiting until everything is perfect to write the perfect book, fine. But at least practice while you wait. Work on a not-perfect book, on a Good Enough book, in the meantime.

If you want your book to be bestselling, riveting, stunning, respected for all the ages ... spend time making yourself into a quality writer capable of producing best-seller material.

How?

Write a book (a.k.a. marry a person) who is a lot like you. Some weak spots. Some gleaming strengths. A real, live, complicated entity. Messy. Some rough edges. And then take what you learn into the next book.

That is how growth occurs; growth isn't usually comfortable, which is why it's called growth and not napping. Growth is change. You can *feel* change. Things move around, detach, reorganize.

When you are perfect, *then* write a perfect book.

For now, allow yourself to write flawed books, and keep feeding your relationship to writing by embracing the process.

You are funny, generous, kind, at times brilliant. You are also afraid, jumpy, easily irritated by loud noises, and weird around cats. You jump to conclusions; you're also capable of wildly fresh insights. You're fun. You're a lot more patient and tolerant of other people's flaws than you used to be. You're a work-in-progress. Just like your book.

When I got seriously stuck writing this book, my editor, Kelly, suggested I go on a kind of second honeymoon. I'd just gotten a divorce from my real-life husband. My parents, both of whom are disabled, were both diagnosed with Alzheimer's disease within months of each other. At work there was a difficult situation in my department. I was *not* in the mood! I could not get myself right to write these chapters. I wanted to impress my colleagues with great brilliance and wit. I wrote like crazy, every day, but my voice was off. Something was broken, out of tune. I couldn't tell how to fix it. It seemed as if the more I tried, the worse things got.

Kelly called me up one day and said, "I think I might have a plan." She became a fabulous marriage therapist for my estranged book project and me. First, she got an extension; that alone lifted so much of the stress and pressure off of me and *Chapter After Chapter.* Then she set it up so it was like I was dating *Chapter.* Every morning, she had me write a journal entry—a kind of love letter addressed to *Chapter After Chapter*. No one would ever see them, she assured me. They were just for practice, just for me. They would never be published. I e-mailed them to her each morning at 10 A.M. In my pretend letters, I wrote about my hard situations, bad writing habits, dark blocks, the people who help, the people who don't. I wrote everything I was afraid to say. I wrote about being naked and poor and jealous. I wrote about the divorce and deceit and literary betrayal and rejection and bad reviews and poor sales and my naïveté and brain injuries and a dreary horrible winter spent not writing. Kelly loved the new stories.

"You're back," she said. She wanted more; *my book* wanted *me* again! In just a few weeks, I was back to writing daily. Writing *Chapter After Chapter* was once again like the fun early stages of dating. Like a new love interest, I'd wake up with the book on my mind. (When you first are falling in love the person or book is never really out of your mind.) I could close my eyes at any point, anywhere, and visualize how *Chapter* would look in my hands. I came home from work not tired, but energized; I ran to my writing desk, the same one I'd been dreading and avoiding for months.

I wrote and wrote and wrote. No commitment. No expectations. This was "just for fun." We each pretended—all three of us, Kelly, the book, and me—that none of this meant anything. We would just see where it went, Kelly assured me. No pressure. No ticking editorial clock. So I had a fling with my book. I quit flogging it, and I learned how to fall in love again. I learned how vital it is to nurture the relationship on a daily basis. I started being nicer to myself and to my book. I quit bad-mouthing it in my head. I brought my book-in-progress flowers, ribbons, and pink Jelly Roll pens.

This book, like most books-in-progress, had a bad run. The smartest thing I did was to stay engaged with *the existing project* instead of going outside to find the Sexy Next Book (see chapter 20). I had a fling. With the book-in-progress.

With the help of a patient, experienced editor, someone who had worked with a lot of other writers like me, I fell in love with my book again.

Instead of focusing on the ways in which I sucked or the ways in which the book sucked (guaranteed methods for assuring mutual destruction), I stepped back and focused on my list: true, smart, kind.

I stepped back in, moved closer to the project, accepting some of my flaws—hasty, scared, disorganized, hurt—and some of my book's flaws: too short, not linear, no ending. In other words, I shortened my want list.

To write a book is to fall in love. To indulge an obsession. In a partnership, you make each other a little better.

Book by book, this is how it goes. What's required is a very generous, tolerant view of the process. There aren't many things that require this kind of long-term devotion and understanding, so don't be too hard on yourself if you don't automatically have these skills. They take years to develop. We're accustomed to classes that last a few months, shows that last a season, vacations that take a week, home renovations that we work on for a week, meals that can be pulled together in under an hour. We don't, as a society, have an enormous amount of experience with long-term endeavors. Hunting season, baseball season, wide-legged jeans, popular books—they're all over so fast.

When you make a commitment, you must be willing to stick it out, to be in it for the long haul. You love your book-in-progress the same way. You're going to be together for a long time. The foundation has to be super solid—your commitment to the book must be total: *I will stay with you and work on this even when it is hard, even when you are difficult and annoying, even when you want to give up on me.*

You keep the passion alive by surprising each other with little things, gifts you know the other will like. "I'm going to try a new exercise to add life to the opening pages." That sounds wonderful! Your book will *love* to be treated this way. "I'm going to introduce a new character," might be a nice surprise, too. You know what to do for your book, and what it would hate, because you spend a lot of quality time together.

You support each other in times of crisis ("We have no ending!"), and you pull together, hunker down. Maybe you go to therapy. Sort of what you and your book are doing right now by completing the exercises in *Chapter After Chapter.*

ON YOUR PAGE: *Exercise 18*

Make a list of the things you are expecting from your book. Each item on your list must be something you yourself have to offer. Maybe your list looks something like this:

Shorter rather than longer

Simple structure

Likes me, and needs me to write it

Humorous but thoughtful

Intense but capable of silliness

Friendly

Doesn't have intimacy issues

ON YOUR PAGE: *Exercise 19*

Writing a book is a long-term relationship, and you already have some strategies for making those kinds of relationships work. What are they? (I would love to see *your* list.) When you are in trouble, relationship-wise, what do you do? For example, you might write:

1. *Check in every day.*
2. *Buy a present.*
3. *Plan fun things to do together.*
4. *Don't always talk about the kids.*
5. *Listen.*

Try for five strategies. Then, write a sentence or paragraph on how you might actively apply that relationship strategy to your book.

When my book turns a cold shoulder to me, I know it's just insecure and unsure—it feels like it doesn't trust me, and maybe it's right! I don't know what the hell I am doing. So I can buy it a present—it loves new office supplies like I love jewelry. Cartridges, a box for all the file cards, really nice paper. Maybe if we can get the first draft done by our one-year anniversary, we can buy a flat-screen monitor. We can pick it out together!

Chapter 19

Taking Baby Along: How to Travel With a Book-in-Progress

I'M AT A WRITING CONFERENCE THIS WEEKEND, IN THE LOVELY Sirata Resort on the beach. It's February, and I live in Michigan; Florida is out there shining in the sun, and I can hardly believe I'm in my dark hotel room, working. When I dashed out for coffee at 6 A.M., I felt the warmth of the shore wind. The Gulf of Mexico was sparkling. But I am locked in Room 3106, in bed with my folders, editing a chapter.

Yesterday on my layover in the airport in Detroit, I reread a stalled chapter and made notes in the margins, ways I could flesh it out, organize the parts, help the opening. I do this with a pen on regular paper.

It's hard to dream up brilliant new stuff when you're out of your element, on the road, about to give a giant presentation to three hundred people. However, I can always work on existing parts of my current project. And right now, I have the subsections of my chapter identified on Post-It notes, and they line my thigh. It looks like I'm going in for surgery, which in a way, I am: I am operating on this chapter.

I want very much to be outside. I'm going to miss my morning run. I'll also miss breakfast with the other writers. I would love so much (I live in *Michigan*!) to be on the beach, lying on my back, feeling the hot sand, the sun on my face.

But it's too hard to start again. I know what will happen if I miss a day. The pain isn't worth it. I have lost too many projects by leaving them unattended.

When laypeople learn how much time writers spend working, they often say, "Oh, you're so disciplined!" But it isn't discipline. For me, it's *fear and desperation.* I don't want the project to slip away because it is too difficult to rein it back in, recapture it.

Writing a new book is like being a parent, I imagine. You just do it. You never make a choice, *Oh, today I think I won't be a parent.* The kid is right in front of you, with needs. No choice for you to make. It's *in* you. You wake up working. You stay in your hotel room changing diapers and lovingly watching the kid sleep, while the other vacationers frolic on beach buggies and shout from the pool.

You have this *baby.*

And the baby is so cool!

Before I go on any trip, I lay out my things. I visualize what I could work on each day, just fifteen minutes a day, and I put the work into folders, each labeled with the day's date. I do not usually take my laptop, because I can never concentrate fully enough to do new work. I take actual hard-copy files, with Post-It note instructions on what to do. I give myself very easy assignments, but there is one for each day of the trip. I always do this. It's simple: Just as I would never leave home without enough underwear for each day, so, too, do I always pack an assignment for every day of the trip. Plus a few extras, a few spares.

Writers know how easy it is to miss a few days post-trip, and then how hard it is—sometimes impossible—to get back into the writing groove after missing four, five, or, heaven forbid, six days. *But we forget.* If I do not write every day of the trip, then I won't write the first day back. Laundry, reconnecting with family, the disaster that is the house—all will get my first attention.

If you miss too many days, your book can change on you. And you change. When you come back together, all of a sudden you are writing in a slightly different key. It's not the same book anymore. And that's *if* you even get back to it.

Nothing is harder in the writing life than trying to start after stopping.

Like a flailing dieter, the new book writer mistakenly thinks: *I can't stick to the plan when I am in Florida—I'll be so busy, my routine will be disrupted, there won't be time, I can only do it when I'm at home.* But healthy, successful dieters bring their own food along. And they have a plan for reentry—before they even leave town, they've blocked out extra gym sessions in their calendar.

Successful writers bring little tiny assignments on their trips. These are tiny tethers. Not whips. Not impossible challenges (*I will begin my new diet on this trip to Paris.*). Small, manageable assignments for staying connected to the work are all you need. You probably won't have enough focus to write brilliant prose for forty-five minutes every morning; you are going to be thinking about the shuttle schedule, the fabulous romance, where to get a magnificent omelet. You will be very distracted, so learn to be realistic. Tethered, but realistic. Long leashes are good.

Even on vacation, pay attention to the book. Take your timer with you. Ten minutes of warm-up and getting ready. Fifteen minutes of focused writing. Lay your things out the night before. Give your book its own little itinerary. If you want to truly finish your book, it must never be farther away from you than your own live human baby. It's always with you; on some level you are always thinking about it. That's the secret to finishing a book.

The pages you produce during these times are less important than the vital fact that you are keeping your connection to your book *alive.* That you re-enter the space of the book every day in a meaningful way.

On your vacation, review the note cards for one of the scenes. Reread one of your Wise Guides. Read the first chapter of your book—don't do anything to it, just read it, every day. Let things percolate, but keep priming the pump. Tiny little micro-movements keep up your connection to the book so that when you re-enter normal life, you re-enter it writing. Dream about the cover for the published book. Write juicy blurbs for yourself. Go to bookstores on your trip and see what's on display. Write a tiny paragraph that scares you.

If you do have to leave your book behind, leave it in good hands. While bringing the book with you is preferable, you can hire someone—a *book sitter*—to watch over it, work on it, tend to its needs while you are away (unless it's an infant book—then you really do have to take it with you).

A book sitter is someone who reads your book and, upon your return, gives you a critique. Or perhaps it's someone who reads a chapter a day and discusses the chapter's strengths and weaknesses with you every afternoon via phone or e-mail while you are on your trip. You can even trade manuscripts with your book sitter. Give him your book; take his with you. It's often easier to do work for someone else than for yourself. You are on task. You are helping another writer. You are tethered to your writing life in a positive, energizing way.

When I take vacation using a book sitter, the best results are achieved by daily check-ins. I send an e-mail to my partner after each section I read, and she sends me notes after each of my chapters. Your muse is fed seductive little treats, and when you return home, you'll slide back into the work. Like you haven't been away at all. Because you haven't.

To write a book is to sustain attention over a long period of time. You're asking no less of your reader.

When I got home to Michigan from the conference, we had a Famous Novelist on our campus for three days, and I was in charge of his visit. He told us about sending a story to a friend for feedback; meanwhile, a prestigious literary magazine, *The Southern Review*, accepted the story. When the friend finally returned the comments, there were some brilliant suggestions. Even though the story was already accepted for publication, the author told *The Southern Review* he would be sending a revision.

When I picked up the Famous Novelist at his hotel to take him to dinner, he was in the lobby, manuscript in his lap. He stood up, slipping the paper into his backpack. He smiled.

"Is that the story?" I said.

He looked a little surprised. "Yes," he said. "The one I was talking about at the session. I'm going over the edits."

I marveled at how smoothly the author moved from *being a writer* into his regular daily life, being a guest, going to dinner. No big drama. This was clearly a man who could travel with a baby, pets, *a manuscript.* His writing life was a folder he just slipped into his backpack. And back out. Each day is filled with these little crevices of time. You can bring your book project with you everywhere you go.

When I dropped him off at the airport, I said, "I can come in with you but I suspect you will enjoy the time alone?"

He smiled gently. "I always have work to do," he said calmly as we shook hands.

And as I drove away, winding out of the airport on a wide curving road that cut through ice-covered fields, a giant snowy owl flew right in front of my truck, fierce, hungry, focused.

It felt like the spirit of the Famous Writer, blessing our writing, pointing toward the work, going home. I told my dear friend Pat about seeing this rare amazing owl at the airport. "That's Jebediah," she said. "He's famous. He's been written up. I've seen him three times."

"Oh," I said. *Other people know about my secret owl?* This is what writer's tips are like. When you discover them on your own you feel special, inspired. When you learn everyone works this way, you feel part of something larger, a member of a particularly interesting group.

Writers who are successful know how to give themselves work (since no one else will). They know how to travel while working and work while traveling. They know what to take. They know what to leave behind.

They practice moving from writing into Real Life and back again.

ON YOUR PAGE: *Exercise 20*

Consider your preparation as a form of trip insurance. Make a pretend to-do list for your book as if you were going on a trip, choosing the tiniest, easiest, simplest things to work on. Think about what you will take with you. Will you take the whole book? A laptop? A hard copy of one chapter? Now imagine your to-do list. What will you work on?

Here's my list from the Florida conference. I made the list several weeks in advance of the trip, when I was in the thick of my memoir about being face blind. I would be gone for five days, so I made six cards—the creating mind likes choices, and it loves being able to say no.

- Write backstory for Mom figure.
- Brainstorm a list of twenty details for the scary brother scene.
- Write a pretend ending, just for practice (repeatable).
- In fifteen minutes, make a list of seventy titles for this book.
- Write the hallway announcement scene.

Some of these are fun, some are hard, some are both. They are like framed photographs you take of your loved ones. They keep you open to your book; they're your lifeline back home.

ON YOUR PAGE: *Exercise 21*

Create a roster of potential book sitters. Collect contact information for three to four writers, or smart, helpful, informed readers, just as you would collect information on dog sitters, babysitters, house sitters. These are *book sitters*. And, don't wait until a few days before your next trip. Contact them now. Ask them if they might be interested in trading work this summer, or over the holidays. Be specific about what they will be asked to do. Go ahead and say, now: "I would like to leave you with the second chapter and five questions I have about the writing in that chapter." Or, "Can we trade rough drafts of our novels? I need a deadline, and my summer vacation is the perfect deadline. I'll give you twenty questions, but feel free to not answer them."

Encourage them to trade work with you. Or work out a payment scale or barter. Unless this person is the godparent of your book (your project does have godparents, doesn't it?), you want to be very professional. And of course, no matter what, you bring them back shells and starfish and tacky T-shirts and coconut patties from the Sirata gift shop.

Chapter 20

Sexy Next Book

When you're working on your book, you will undoubtedly be tempted by Fresh Start Sirens. Gorgeous, tantalizing new book ideas will arrive, making juicy promises.

These new ideas are going to pop up, assuring you a baggage-free new beginning. They want to lure you away from your existing project, those boring bad days of writing month after month, no end in sight. The Sexy Next Book idea always promises it will never be difficult; it will never be a burden. It says it's *way, way* more publishable, plus more fun! It whispers, *Take me now. I'm all yours.*

When this happens: Run. Run as fast as you can in the other direction. *Do not get involved* with this book!

Sexy Next Book ideas are most likely to pop up when you're in the middle, in the winter of your current book. But, like a bad cold, they can happen any time. When the work isn't going well. When the work is going great. When you're through working for the day, driving to the grocery store to get stuff for dinner. *Pow!* A great new book idea lands in your lap.

No.

Do not go there. You're already taken.

So what do you do with this energy?

Do you harness it?

Play it out, see where it takes you?

Can you save it, bottle it up?

Do you stop, take notes for a few days, commit the new idea to paper, and then save it for later?

When do you put your current project aside? How do you tell if the Sexy Next Book is *better*?

My writing friend Janelle confesses to more than a few flings. In real life she is a devoted spouse and a fabulous, generous mother to her son, Will. In her writing life, she, like all of us, can be quite flighty, quite the flirt. Her Fresh Book Sirens always arrive just when she is on the verge of a breakthrough in her existing project. She'll say, "Heather, I'm so done with this sister book! I've worked on it for five years! I got this idea for a Galveston novel about a flood. A saga, really. I can see the whole thing. I'm shelving the sister book. I'm doing the flood. I'm on my way to the library right now. I've always wanted to write a saga!" She's talking fast, like a teenager in love with the football star who has just asked her out.

Talking Janelle down is like getting a cat out of a tree. I have to act cool. Come out with her favorite food. Speak softly. Act like I'm not desperate to get her down from there.

I start by pointing out that she has *not* worked on the sister book—which is really good and nearly done—for five years but rather for two summers (intensively) and one fall (four evenings out of seven), and that these periods were not consecutive, so it feels like five years but it's really hardly one. I point this out by saying, "You're so *into* the sister book now! It's so good! There's work to be done. Stay with it. Then do the flood."

I walk past her tree like I have all the time in the world. This crazy Galveston fling, with its promise of glitter and ease. Treacherous! Sexy Next Books are *unknowns*. And, like every new relationship, fun and full of possibility. No wonder it is so easy to get sucked in.

Every book in your head seems easier than what you're doing now.

When you're writing a book, you're essentially married.

There will be Sexy Next Book ideas wiggling and swaggering their way down the sidewalk, back and forth in front of your house, "Pick me! I'm hot! I'm fun! I'm easy!" Or, in the case of the Galveston novel, "I'm brilliant! I involve libraries! I'm your ticket to literary accolades!" New book ideas arrive in adorable blue convertibles. They do not come with seatbelts.

Just say no.

You can appreciate them, briefly, and maybe make a little note card, take down their phone number. Tuck that little card into a box or folder titled "Future Book Ideas." Every writer I know has this box or folder or drawer. A kind of little black book.

To write your book, you need total focus. You need to write one book at a time. You need to finish what you start. That's how you learn to write a book. If you keep starting, you're teaching yourself, quite handily, to be great at starting books. There are thousands of people in this category. No more are needed. Teach yourself to finish books. There's a lot of room for finishers.

Realize that if you turn your back on your current book, your current book *will turn its back on you*. If you betray your project for the Fresh Book Sirens, don't expect it to instantly take you back when the Sexy Next Book flirts off, disappears into the sunset, hardly giving you the time of day. Commitment isn't always fun. You stay to build something larger, something that lasts, something serious and good.

However ... it is okay to look. It's even healthy to look. I am being entirely literal.

If you're sideswiped by a Sexy Next Book idea, if you're tantalized by Fresh Book Sirens, don't feel guilty for looking. Just don't look for too long. Give yourself one day.

You get one day to do a Sexy Next Book Check (see the exercise at the end of the chapter). If you're cautious and intentional, if you parse your energy and attention very carefully, you can chat with a Sexy Next Book without losing your current project, without ticking it off permanently. This takes finesse. Practice. If you're smart, you'll be able to return to this new idea—the rose will not turn to ash—in a year or so when you have sent the current project off to agents and editors.

But you get no more than one day for this introduction.

You can *dream* a book this way without being disloyal. But be careful. You can't do this all the time and sustain the pure unadulterated energy you need to feed the book project that is underway. Once a month, maybe, allow yourself to look around. If you spend more time dreaming about the *other* book than you do working hard on the current one, you will drain the life right out of the marriage. It will suffer. No one will be happy.

You learn by finishing. Even if you picked a bad book idea, in most cases you will learn more by seeing it through than you will by chasing after that Sexy Next Book idea.

Go back to your current project, your Main Squeeze.

Keep going back.

And if you do get lured away, don't be too hard on yourself. Just trust your instinct, and learn what you can from every experience.

For instance, Janelle did put the sister book down in order to read two centuries of Texas history, flood narratives, and Galveston geography. The new relationship with the Galveston book lasted into the summer, then Creep set in and they started seeing less and less of each other. Janelle eventually returned to the sister book, wiser, more committed, but not until a whole year had passed. (She was grieving and healing from the Galveston novel.)

Sometimes, though, the Fresh Book Sirens are right to lure you away.

Last year when I was at work on the best novel I have drafted to date, a Sexy Next Book courted *me*. I stopped, smack in the middle of my novel and gave my full attention, for one whole day, to this new project knocking at my door, bringing me treats, refusing to leave me alone, calling all hours of the day and night. This flirty book turned out to be my face-blind memoir. After spending four hours writing the book in a sentence, a paragraph, a page, ten pages, thirty pages (see the exercise at the end of the chapter)—I found myself, one month later, shacked up with the project! We are still together, and it was the right thing to do. I simply had to write the face-blind memoir *right here right now* because I was in the midst of undergoing the medical treatments, and I was reading all the scientific research anyway. The book came to me whole.

The novel is *pissed.* Rightly so. I abandoned it. I might have even killed it. It will take me a long time to earn its trust again; I may be essentially starting over. But, I believe I made the right choice. Working on the face-blind memoir has made me happier than anything else.

This is the writing life. Hard choices, limited time, developing an instinct of what to trust and when to take a leap of faith.

ON YOUR PAGE: *Exercise 22*

Devote one full day to your book. Your actual book-in-progress. You need to spend six to eight hours of uninterrupted, focused attention—and it will send the sexy, flirty new idea skittering off the dance floor and back to the sidelines. This is Vow Renewal 101. Work on your book for one full day.

If you can't do that, then go ahead and have the fling. But limit it: You can have one full day to decide if throwing away your life's work, your long-term relationship, the book you have been working so hard on, is worth it. If your Sexy Next Book thrills at the idea of having a day with you all to itself, that's a good sign, but you need more. You need a full commitment. You need promises.

Ask the Sexy New Book: *Can you state your whole self in one sentence?* Your Sexy Next Book will ramble on, and that's okay. Be sure to listen. Write down everything. Then, keep at it, asking follow-up questions: *But what is the single most important concept you offer? What are you really, essentially, about?*

This will take a few hours. You're trying to get the *whole* book in one sentence. After all, you can't make a decision like this based only on *thoughts* of a Sexy Next Book. Get it down to a sentence. Then decide.

Chapter 21
Braids

We start so many books. Writing for twenty, fifty, seventy pages, all high-hopes and happy-plan, and then stopping. Bottoming out. In the middle. Again and again.

One reason so many books-in-progress die on the vine is because there isn't enough spark, enough energy in the original design to drive the project all the way through the middle and close the deal.

The middle of a book is often compared to a lonely and vast desert that the writer has to hike across. It's easy to get lost. It's easy to give up. There are monsters in the middle—working too fast, not working daily, wanting to be done, getting kind of bored.

To get across the middle, your work must involve some element of discovery—something you have to *figure out as you write*. Otherwise, your writing will feel canned, preplanned, flat. Like stale popcorn.

This is where braiding comes in. Most people have known about braiding since they were little kids. Our hair has been braided on our very heads; we've braided doll hair and strands of string and strips of paper. Remember those pine needle zippers we used to make? Humans *naturally* braid things. A braid is strong and interesting. And it makes for a sound book structure. Braids save you from losing momentum, and they keep you on track and make your work instantly more layered and complex in a simple and easy-to-do way.

Braided books (or articles or stories) are made up of three or four strands or story lines. Three seems to be the ideal number (for hairstyling, for book writing). Instead of slogging through one story line and then flatlining somewhere in the middle, braids help you mix it up. You tell three stories, bit by bit. The juxtapositions lend life and surprise, tension and drama. You work in small manageable sections, folding in new material. Things stay fresh and lively and manageable.

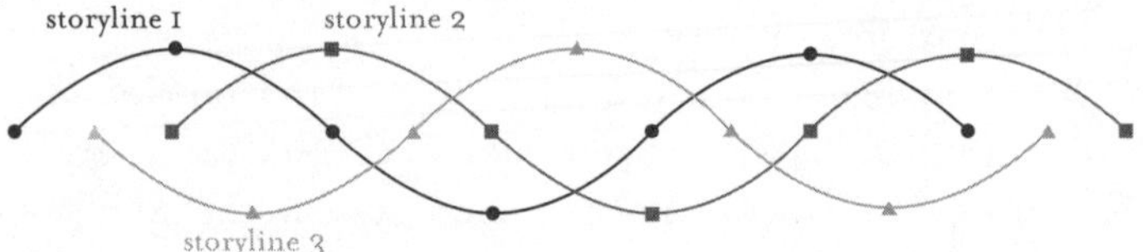

For example, in a braided novel about divorce and reconciliation, you would tell the story of the divorce a little at a time, interspersing the teenage daughter's first romance with the story of the live-in mother-in-law and her crazy scheme to bring fame to the town. You tell three smaller, simpler stories—one of loss, one of love, and one of generation—in small, bite-size pieces. One section at a time, from each of the three "source" stories. It is much easier to work this way.

To braid, imagine yourself going through family photos from three different trips. The Bahamas honeymoon photos, the photos from the Indian mounds trip when the kids were babies, and photos of your mother last time you visited. You take the most interesting photos from each trip or strand, and lay them out to tell a story. Start with the Bahamas kissing photo. Then choose one from the mounds trip: the one with the kids all in a heap, laughing, but Shelly is yanking Em's hair, hard. Then your mother, alone, in the doorway, the light on her face so she looks like she did when she was a child. A lot like Shelly, come to think of it.

And then you cycle through again, until you have enough images to tell a story. With three sources feeding your book, it's easier to keep things fresh and alive.

For fiction or a memoir, braid with images from each of your three story lines and you come up with photo-like moments: 1-2-3, 1-2-3. For nonfiction, you choose topics or approaches. A refrigerator repair manual has three kinds of information: stuff you need to observe carefully with your eyes (is the ice buildup clear or snowy?); tools and how you use them; and basic diagrams for how the fridge is put together. The manual's sections cycle through these three kinds of information. You work in little blocks.

Last year, I judged a major national essay contest. It was an interesting experience, because only about 10 percent of the pieces even remotely worked. Most fell flat because they were *about one thing*, something the writers had already decided the pieces would be about. No room to wiggle around, get lost, wonder about the deeper nature of things, wander off to the side a bit, discover the interesting not-before-noticed thing. Those authors each had *one* thing to say, and gosh darn it they were going to say it come hell or high water.

Sermons, rants at teenagers, lectures for college students (especially freshmen), even love letters—these may work like that. But not art.

Art relies on surprise. In order to engage the reader (and yourself as a writer), you have to braid. You can't be confusing, but you can't spell it all out, either. The human mind, when it reads, needs something to figure out. You can't just go on and on about the refrigerator compressor, the history of the compressor, the likes and dislikes of the compressor, particular compressor models.

You need *more than one thing* going on at a time. And you don't need to know how everything will work out. When you braid, happy accidents occur—the image of your mother's friends in the retirement home singing off-key for her birthday, all of them crying, inspires you to write a terrible child's birthday scene. You would have never thought of it without the prompting of the braiding activity; often, these inspired surprises produce some of our best writing.

In my face-blind memoir, I have three braids, three photo albums to draw from. Childhood. Recognition problems because of my neurological disorder. And the story of my marriage and divorce. I trust in the possibilities of how the stories will refract off each other. When I tell the story of my Florida childhood, divorce will be in some of the images. Marriage is about recognizing another person, deeply, profoundly. My braids twine in and out of each other. Coming of age, an illness, a marriage—the book *teaches me* what it is about as I write it. That's the best way to write a book: to follow a structure that allows you to discover wise insights, images, and a natural organization as you go along.

If you are concerned about organization, try dividing your book into three sub-stories, three sub-themes. You can write each one straight through. Or you can divide and conquer, working on each strand a little bit at a time. Most braiders do a little of both.

I asked my students to do a braided essay using completely unrelated topics; the only requirement was that they write about something that mattered a whole lot to them. For Braid One, Christian chose to write about his experience in a tug-of-war ritual at our college, which takes place over the Black River. For Braid Two, he excerpted journal entries from his great-great-great-great uncle Pieter Damstra, one of the first Dutch settlers of our present-day community. For Braid Three, Christian told stories of terrible dates from his sophomore year, where he said really stupid things, drove women away, or just got bored and broke up for no real reason.

It's one of the best student pieces I have ever read.

In class, everyone praised Christian for his deep connections and insights, and for the subtle patterns he drew between relatives, dating, and tug-of-war. Christian smiled at us and said, "What patterns?"

He didn't see that when his ancestor talked about how his wife, Albatross, was really annoying on the boat on the way over—which came up the Black River, the very river over which Christian tugged!—there was an echo, a refraction, a little mirror in the writing. He didn't see what the class could see in his piece: Love is a tug-of-war. Ancestors pull you back. Christian thought he was being lazy and cheating by using the journal excerpts because he had written less than the other students. His old Dutch relatives worried all the time that they weren't working hard enough, too. I could go on and on, and in class, we did.

I now teach the braid in every class, and I have started using it as a revision strategy. Many pieces that aren't working are actually fine—they're just not complex enough. They are the Braid A, and they will not come to life, no matter what you do, until you spark-feed them with a Braid B, and then a Braid C.

This is true for articles, poems, essays, novels, books, nonfiction, romance novels, everything.

Every episode of *Friends* is braided.

Notice your conversations with your friends. Braided. Notice your favorite video games. What are the braids, or strands?

You can be a little aware of the connections, but leave lots of room for discovery. After the draft is up and running, you can shape and bend—add another scene at the tug-of-war event, for example, where your own parents stand on the banks and cheer as you grunt and pull a rope over the river where your great-greats landed in Michigan.

You can steer and bend and shape. But braid first.

And watch the sparks start flying.

Good writing has layers. It does more than one thing. It leaves room for the reader to go *Aha!*

ON YOUR PAGE: *Exercise 23*

Look at your book in terms of a braid structure. Have a friend or writing-group partner (since it's hard to rethink your work on the structural level) separate out three story lines. You may need to create a new line to complicate your story, or you may want to promote a line from within the existing structure to more emphatically triangulate what is already there.

Do a new outline based on this structure and limit yourself to very small flashes or glimpses—like photographs or snapshots—for the entire length of each strand.

If this doesn't work the first time, try it again. Or, try it with a different project, not the one you are working on now, just to introduce your brain to this new kind of structure. If you are one of the many people who think in terms of "the next three books I want to write," you are a good candidate for braiding.

Chapter 22
The Little Editor Who Can't Stop

I HAVE A FREE-SPEAKING, VERY WELL-INFORMED ENTITY within me: the bossy Little Editor who can't stop "helping." She—I will use that pronoun in this chapter since mine is a she, and *she* cares about pronouns, political correctness, and everything else to do with being perfect—is with me every step of the way.

It turns out a lot of writers have these insistent perfection seekers lurking within them. Little Editors seem helpful and comforting, like all bossy people do at first—*Oh, I can fix that for you!* She makes you feel that without her, you would suck so bad that shooting yourself in the head would make sense. Thus, you cling to her. She hovers over every sentence. You aren't going to make a mistake, not with her around to help. She makes sure you write one perfect sentence at a time. *Wait until Little Editor gives the okay*. You never finish anything because whatever you write isn't perfect, isn't up to her standards. She keeps telling you what to do. *It's not there yet. You can do better. I'll show you how.*

She is desperate to keep her job, like that suck-up at your place of employment, so she's always "on" whenever you're at the writing desk. She's so convincing, so good at grammar and perfection, you believe her when she whispers, *Without me, you're dead*.

The exact opposite is true.

In Deborah Tannen's book *You're Wearing That?: Understanding Mothers and Daughters in Conversation*, the mother is often surprised when the daughter reacts negatively to a comment. "You've slimmed down!" is met with a hostile stare, when the mother was just saying, "You look great." Tannen explains that this occurs because there's also a meta-message in the mother's statement—"You had some weight to lose, good job in becoming slimmer." The mother isn't wrong, but she needs to keep her mouth shut. The daughter isn't wrong for reacting negatively, but she needs to understand the mother's good intentions.

The whole book reminded me of the way we talk to ourselves while we are writing. *You're writing that?* I hear in my head, day after day after day, sentence after sentence. It's *her* again.

"What's wrong with it?" I'm tempted to say to this little voice. But I'm already hurt, a little ashamed; it's too late. The damage is done.

The Little Editor does mean well. She knows you are terrified of making a fool of yourself, and she's truly trying to help. It's just that the fear she induces is not conducive to *writing*.

And, of course, that doesn't mean your Little Editor is wrong. She is absolutely right. The mother in the above example? One hundred percent right. The daughter did want to lose ten pounds, she talked about it, she worked hard at it, she's happy she looks good. But a comment on weight (or clothes or hair or the raising of one's children) may be interpreted as criticism. When you're trying to have a nice lunch, or write a chapter, those comments aren't helpful.

Do not try to get it perfect before going on. You won't be able to go on long enough to finish a book. No one can stand that kind of "help" day after day. So what do you do?

One friend of mine treats the voices of commentary in his head as a senate. He divides them into one hundred *different* commentators. He writes a sentence, and if he can get a majority—even fifty-one of the guys—to say, "Sounds good enough to me," he goes ahead. He doesn't ask for a full senate vote on every sentence, because that is what we call gridlock, folks, and there *is a country to run here (and a book to write).* You gotta move the bills through. You gotta combine hunks of stuff into one bill—or you will never get anywhere.

Be prepared to hear screaming when you vote the Little Editor off the island and consult the senators instead.

She is getting fired, after all. You cannot expect someone who gets laid off for expertly doing her job to go quietly or say thank you.

She is going to *freak out.*

Do not confuse her with you.

She has to go.

You can't write a book if the Little Editor is in charge. You can't write a book if she is even in the same county.

Editing while writing blocks your creativity. It keeps you from immersing in the messy chaotic depths of truth, wisdom, images, complicated interactions. Editing while writing ensures you don't grow too much, too quickly. It's safe. Safe like training wheels.

Retaining the Little Editor who can't stop "helping" is like clinging to your mom's apron strings well into your forties.

Real live editors work for *publishers.* These people are paid to tell you where you have gone astray. This is done *after you have written the book.* That's the proper time for this kind of editing.

Right now your job is writing. Not editing.

Write. Write badly, write beautifully, write at night. Stay up way too late, ruin your skin, forget to shave, grow your hair long *at your age*, and write and write and write and write. Make a mess. Don't clean it up. Do it your way. She's not the boss of you. This is *your* book.

Tell the Little Editor to bother someone else. You know she means well, but if she wants a job at all, ever, she needs to vanish until you summon her after your book is finished. Tell her it's going to be a while.

ON YOUR PAGE: *Exercise 24*

Intermediate version: Write really badly for ten minutes without stopping. Write by hand (the Little Editor loves word processing, pressed khaki pants, self-cleaning ovens—you know her tastes!). Make mistakes. Write fast. You win if you do not make sense, if you have incomplete sentences, if you gush, lie, make notes for other topics in the margins because thoughts are coming so fast. For those of you with highly developed super-effective internal editors, consider repeating this daily, as a warm-up, before your writing session.

Advanced version: Write a letter informing your Little Editor who can't stop of her immediate termination. Fire her now. Let her find work somewhere else. Does she even need work? Is this the Wicked Witch? Melt her. It's an excellent task to do in a partnership or small group: Read the letter where you fire her and give just cause—stuff that will hold up in court, like mental abuse, consistent lying, stealing ideas, etc. This firing of someone working on the inside, someone who is consistently sabotaging you and everything you work so hard for, is cause for celebration!

Chapter 23

Naked

I AM IN THE SAUNA WITH MY WORKOUT PARTNERS, VERA AND Lisa. We are wrapped in towels. We're telling our secrets. The cedar room is small, dimly lit, and it feels like the safest place on campus. We're telling our stories about our parents, our children, our bosses, and our exes, the annoying people we know, how hard *we* try to be not-annoying. The hurt feelings, misunderstandings, the difficulty of trying to always do the right thing, trying to be polite, correct, nice—our stories and troubles get steamed out of us, soaking into the wood, and we're feeling a lot better.

Outside the sauna, the sound of the shower whooshes, hard water hitting hard tile.

"Oh, no," Vera says.

"Yup," Lisa says.

The door to the sauna opens and stays open. The girls come in, one at a time, holding the door open and grabbing their towels, which we've placed neatly on the floor. They frown at us. I shiver.

We are naked under our towels.

They are in bathing suits.

You see, there's a war going on in the Hope College women's locker room. A war over appropriate locker room costuming standards. For our students, the sauna is a giant towel warmer and changing room. Sweaty from basketball or track practice, they come in one at a time and change in the dark closet that is the sauna. They leave their towels spread out on the empty benches. They change into swimsuits then hit the showers. *In their swimsuits.* They don't like naked people in their sauna; it ticks them off and messes up their routine. We're wrapped in towels, mind you—decent but oh, so close to the edge.

"Can y'all close the door, maybe?" I say.

The girl holding the sauna door open stares at me blankly and then looks away. Another dashes in, as though she is entering a house of ill repute by force, gathers up all the rest of the towels, and they both dash out, finally letting the door close.

"Thanks!" I yell through the wood.

This happens every single day. It will take hours for the sauna to get warm again; our conversation is frozen.

The girls do not have what we have: varicose veins, stretch marks, bad scars, weird creasy knee skin, multiple chins, sagging breasts, dimply forty-one-year-old butts.

We have all those things.

"They do not want us in here," Vera says. "We embarrass them."

At first I doubted this. Wouldn't these beautiful girls feel no shame in being naked? Haven't we all been naked like this for years? They're perfect, lovely, strong. They can't be *naked in a shower?*

Evidently, you do not shower naked. Not at my school.

But we radical professors do it anyway. Like Elsie, a swimmer in her late seventies who has a body as beautiful as a map, and Diane, a swimmer in her eighties who moves naked through the locker room like a gentle animal, clear and focused and delicate and amazing.

This whole not-being-naked thing is exactly like writing. *Sometimes we write as though we are wearing a swimsuit in the shower.* Sometimes we are so scared of the truth or of offending people with our very presence, our strength, our energy, our self, that we cover up. We all like to fit in. If the other girls are in swimsuits, well, by golly, we should be, too.

Writers: If you aren't naked, you aren't doing it right.

If you aren't willing to show your sags, your scars, your beautiful arms, the small of your perfect back—your writing voice is going to keep sliding away from you. It will be clear to everyone that you are *faking it.*

You don't have to reveal all. Vera and Lisa and I are not in there slinking around like aging pole dancers, *everything* on display.

But we *are* naked. We are truthful. Towels appropriately arranged. We are not aware of each other's bodies. We are not concerned with nakedness. We are totally focused on one thing in the dim light of the sauna: *our stories.*

A book does not get written when an author fears her own voice, her own perfect body, her unique truth, her sense of what is right and true and normal. "It's a LOCKER ROOM!" I want to shout to the swimsuit girls. But Vera won't let me.

"We're scary enough as it is," she says.

Once, I wrote a whole draft of a book wearing a swimsuit in a shower. My voice was forced, and I was trying to be like everyone else. I didn't like the feeling I had when I was writing, but the story looked okay, it appeared I was on the right track. I was working hard not to offend anyone. (Hint: That's a clue that you're wearing your swimsuit.)

Get a towel. You can be naked and protected. But that essential vulnerability has to be present.

Here's the thing: When you're in the writing sauna, you have to tell the truth as you know it. You have to bare your soul and expose the good and the bad. Don't protect yourself with false fronts, false selves, and officially sanctioned book material. Your work is to reveal *what is not easily seen.* Yes, you are naked, but this is the exact right place to be naked. You're *supposed* to be naked. It's wrong to just warm your towels in the writing sauna, to dip in and out, letting out the heat for everyone else. A book is, after all, a locker room for true human experience. It's supposed to be honest.

Be *appropriately naked*. Connect with others through what you say to each other in a secret room where the door stays closed so the heat doesn't escape. That's what a book is—a private communication between two people (multiplied by x). You can wear a small towel. But underneath, you have to tell the truth. And you have to deal with the fact that there are a lot of swimsuit-in-the-shower people in this world, and they want you to *not do this.* They want you to *be like them*.

You can fend them off by writing your book to your most trusted friends. To your Vera and Lisa. To whomever it is that you can bare your soul honestly and fairly. To people who raise you up, whose wisdom is safe, whose experience and judgment you trust. I had a framed photo of a trusted person to whom I wrote every word of *Georgia Under Water*, my collection of short stories. By looking at his photo, I could always tell if I was lying, cheating, rushing, going too slow.

It was a perfect mixed-gender sauna experience. Not always comfortable. But always real. Always true.

I don't know that those unsure feelings ever go away. That fear of revealing the wrong thing is always present in the sauna and in book writing. *This will really kill them. I can't be this person and still be loved! If they find out about this, I'll be not welcome in this room.* Those are just normal *I'm naked!* thoughts. Everyone has them.

Writers are the people who sit smack-dab in the middle of *the mess.* Trying to keep a clear enough head in the midst of the fear to *focus on the story.*

When I'm writing in my true voice, telling the things I'm on the planet to witness and put into words, I feel I'm naked on stage, exposed, while a whole bunch of people in clothes are looking at me and I have no idea what they think.

However, in the wings backstage, is my posse, people who are engaged in the same activity. My sauna people. I look to them—my editor; other writers I adore and respect like Lorraine, Amy, Debra, Jackie and Elaura; my most trusted friends like Vera and Lisa; my best readers, Ann and Janis; the fine students who try to do this same kind of work—Bethany, Nicole, Matt, Kristin, Ashley, Elena, Christian, Laura. Underneath small towels they are naked, too. We have extreme respect for terror and love and truth. I write to them.

Books give us greater protection from the elements. They steer us through the shark-infested waters of petty politics and destructive social norms—the ones that do not keep us safe but just keep us down. Books are how we see *past* fear: fear of being naked, fear of being wrong, fear of telling, fear of losing friendship, fear of losing locker room status.

Some people aren't going to want you to do this work. They will ask you questions that make you cry. They're going to ruin your day. They're going to say, "You're doing it wrong. Who do you think you are?" And you will question and doubt and fear. *Should I be in a swimsuit like the others?*

Writing naked means writing the way you talk to your two closest friends when the door is closed, and your eyes are closed, and you are comfortable naked under your towel, and the showers aren't running, and no one's about to come in, and *you are not afraid.*

Write quietly and honestly and purely; get that energy in your book. Write naked, but be smart about it. Write to those who say to you: *Tell me more.* Steer toward those who gently question, *Is this the whole story? What are you not saying? Are you afraid? Close the door. Keep the heat in. You're safe here. Your words will never leave this room. What is really going on?*

The writing is your cloak. The words are your threads. They reveal exactly the right amount. Focus on making them beautiful.

ON YOUR PAGE: *Exercise 25*

What are you not writing about in your book because the swimsuit girls will completely freak out? Start a list and keep adding to it.

Remember, a lot of self-censoring you can't even see because social forces are so powerful. Watch your motivations. If you list something out of anger, fear, or hoping to shock and awe, maybe that goes on another list. Practice paying attention to what you are covering up just because everyone else is covering it up, *not for any good reason.*

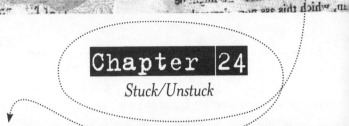

Chapter 24
Stuck/Unstuck

THERE ARE THREE MAGIC WORDS WHEN YOU'RE WRITING A book: *Keep starting again.*

You're never going to get to a place where you are up on some stuck-free platform—that place doesn't exist. There's no superior Writers Hall of Fame where you just sit around behind glass totally mind-melded to your work, writing books with ease.

Writing is a process of working until you get stuck, then figuring out how to get unstuck, starting again, and getting stuck again.

Stuck. Unstuck. Stuck. Unstuck.

That's writing. Writing a book is a cycle of starting agains. It's like surfing. You look for waves, trying to choose a good one, knowing you'll land on shore after the sweet but always brief ride. Then you paddle out again. Ride in. Paddle out. Wait. Stuck on flat water. Digging in, using your eyes, looking for where the waves are likely to break.

Diving into something that you know has this essential crashing-on-the-shore rhythm—stop, start, stop, start—is not for the faint of heart.

It helps to have a stockpile of strategies, tools you can use to get unstuck.

Recently, I was at a weekend conference where I desperately wanted to go to a session called "Plot With Post-Its!"

According to the program, the presenter, a well-published novelist, would explain how she used color-coded Post-It notes to make her books. I wanted to know the Post-It secret, but I was teaching a course during her time slot. Then I remembered: While you can get good ideas about process and technique, *other people's methods won't get you started and they won't get you unstuck.* You have to find your own way.

Try to notice what *you* actually do to get yourself unstuck. What did you do that got you moving again? Articulate for yourself *what exactly happened.* It's really hard to reach for the right tool when you're in the midst of being stuck. Prepare your tools in advance. Keep them clean and handy. Know the strategies that help you most. Here are four that many writers try because they are simple and easy to use.

Make a List

The unconscious writing mind, the place where all the good stuff comes from, likes choices, freedom, and surprise. Our best work comes from that place just behind the front brain—a place that is a little wild, a little chaotic, a little hard to manage. Lists are your bridge into that place.

When you're stuck, when you're not sure what to write, make a list of options. Chances are good that by the time you get to twenty or six or eighty-seven, you will have figured out the next most right step.

Not sure what to put in your scene at the big basketball game? How to write it, what to do? Make a list of everything you see, everything that could be there. All the little details and images and key actions. Water bottles, lip sweat, Joe's untied Nike, the golden retriever that walked onto the paint.

Need a title? List one hundred in seventeen minutes. If you're not sure what the next line in your poem is, list seven options. The front brain likes repetition, security, the known, the predictable. It's happy making lists, and when you're stuck, you have a front-brain takeover problem. Give it something else to do to get it off your back.

Lists are your springboard to surprise. You can make a list for anything. One hundred words when you need a perfect word. One hundred titles (so you get forty and three are pretty good). Potential scenes between the mom and the son? List eighty-five things they could argue over. Force yourself to make lists—you're feeding your creative brain. Many of the exercises in this book are simple list-making activities. When you're stuck, you forget you have choices. Lists give you back your power to choose.

See, Don't Know

Lawyers, essayists, speechwriters, and philosophers work by ideas, thoughts, mental knowing. That's good work. It's just not what we do.

Practice the difference between *seeing* and *knowing*. Most stuck writers are thinking too hard; they forget to envision what the reader will see in her mind's eye as she reads.

Artists work in sensory images. We are sculptors, painters, *makers*. Our work must appeal at the sensual level. When you're stuck, notice what happened right before the stuck-time. Did you lose track of the sensory world of your book? Are you trying to *think* it into being?

Go back to *seeing*.

When artists are learning to draw, their teachers chant at them: "Draw what you see, not what you know." Our front brain comes up with great schemes, shortcuts, really smart-sounding alternate plans. "You want to draw a tree? I know a tree!" the front brain chats, like an annoying sits-in-the-front-row straight-A dweeb. "I can do a tree! Let me!"

Well ...

Yeah. You can draw a *cartoon* of a tree. A *generalized* tree. A *symbol* for a tree.

Great artists work from life. They draw an actual experience of a tree, a visual rendering. Sometimes green parts *look* orange. The oak on the left side of your driveway has a whole different personality from the right-side oak.

My friend Amy Young, whom I was privileged to work with on our book for children, says she can distinguish between illustrators who work from life and those who work from photographs. She can tell from their art what they are looking at: something "real" or something "not real." Something alive or something third-hand.

For your writing to get unstuck, you need to work from life—and that doesn't mean just from actual personal experience. You need to write what you see. After all, your mind's eye can see *anything you want*. And the place you write from shouldn't be a picture you *know* from television or movies or books. Don't listen to that annoying over-eager front brain, who always says, "Put this in! Do it like this!" Write from a "real" place, a place you can mentally picture.

You see in 3-D, in color, and you can only see one thing at a time. In fact, you often don't know what you will see next as you play the movie of your scene in your head. You want to have a sensory visual experience, just like when you dream or retell a story to your wife or your daughter. This is seeing with your mind's eye.

Notice Your Rhythm

Getting unstuck is a mental game, a head job, an inside deal. Pay attention to how you work best. Learn your own rhythm, your ups and downs. Repeat what works. Sound obvious? Many of my writing students walk around thinking either *I'm inspired*! or *I don't feel like writing*! and they have no idea why.

They're stuck *because they haven't been writing.* But they think exactly the opposite: They haven't been writing because they are stuck.

Inspiration isn't random or quixotic. Smart writers learn how to conjure it by paying attention to what happens right before and during a good writing session. If I write three days in a row, I can count on the next four, five, and six days as being productive. If I miss a day, when I start up again it will be either really great (my unconscious has been at work) or really awful and depressing (I lost my thread). If I miss more than three days, I know it will take me three days of writing, of staying with it even though it is sucking horribly, to get my rhythm again.

It's the same for athletes and musicians and artists and parents who are away from their kids. It takes about as much time as you were away to get back to where you were. Knowing that, knowing how painful it is to write through these bad days, is what makes me very motivated to not miss many days. My friends say, "How do you do it, every day? You're so disciplined."

I am not disciplined. I keep working in order to avoid painful consequences.

I know how much I have to write in order to write fairly smoothly, without angst and drama—two hours a day, missing very few days. Noticing this rhythm has helped me to get unstuck and stay unstuck for longer periods of time.

The next time you're stuck, notice how much you've been writing on that day, that week, that month. Has there been any change in your rhythm? How has that affected the stuckness? Go ahead and write anyway. It will probably be terrible writing, but that's not important—you just need to write so you can notice what you are doing. What's hard? What does it feel like? What exactly *can't* you do during this stuck period?

Attention to your process feels weird and counterproductive. But when you notice what's going on before you're stuck, you can build little rhythms and structures to break your fall.

Change Location

This past March, I was working steadily on not one book but two. Everything was in perfect balance—parents stable, friendly ex-husband, healthy dog, house heated, bills paid, car running well. I had a great rhythm going. And then ... one of my books jumped the tracks—I'd written it while wearing that metaphorical swimsuit in the shower—and I knew I had to start over.

Meanwhile the building I work in, good old Lubbers Hall, circa 1922, was slated for a renovation. I have a dreadful dust allergy. When the construction company took down the ceiling tiles on the first floor, I started sneezing uncontrollably all day long. By the time they got to the second floor, I was coughing and infected, peering through red squinty eyes at my students, some of whom were coated with a fine milky dust. And by the time the workers attacked the third floor, where my office is located, I had to get out.

I felt like a spotted owl in the midst of a logging site.

My little nest was moved to a new location—no window, no view, a strange pulsing heating system, cement block walls. Everything was messed up and had to be sorted out. I lost things. It was time consuming and distracting. I had to write with bare-bones references, out of a few boxes, and without all my precious *stuff* in all its special *places.*

But the dislocation unstuck me.

All the old bad energy was gone. The troubled manuscript came out of its packing crate fresher and fuller, in better shape than I thought it was. It seemed to just *blossom* in its new office space. It had room to grow.

Moving a book-in-progress is like fluffing the pillows or shaking out your pockets or cleaning out the junk drawer. Next time you're stuck, move.

It could be a little move, like from your regular writing room to a coffee shop where you won't be bothered for two hours. Or to the library in the evening where you can write for an hour. Write outside; write in an empty classroom. Move your office to another part of the house. Get in your car, drive to a town thirty miles away, sit in a parking lot, and write for an hour. You'll be stunned at how many great new ideas you get *driving back home to the old nest.*

Making lists, looking more closely at the experience your words create for the reader, noticing your own writing rhythm, and moving your camp to a new campsite are quick and easy ways to get unstuck, to liven things up. You will find your own ways; let your writing life teach you what to do.

ON YOUR PAGE: *Exercise 26*

Take what is useful from this chapter and make your own list based on what you know about how you work best. Do some fast freewriting, or discuss this topic with your writing group.

Take notice of when you have a good writing session. Think about what you did before the session began and what you did after it was over. After a week or so of observing how you work, make a list of guidelines. Title it "For Best Results." Write, paint, draw, or type your list. Laminate it and hang it by your computer. On one side of your desk are your Six Wise Guides, and on the other side is this nifty tailor-made how-to manual that contains the secrets to running your writing life smoothly. Here's one writer's list:

1. Intend to write. (No thinking; no talking.)
2. Tune soul. (Poetry is best. Also prayer, music, meditation—see books and CDs on shelf.)
3. Align the mind and the body with breathing for two minutes. Constructive rest. Stretches. (Lie on back, pull knees to chest six times, one at a time, breathing.)
4. If I didn't make a game plan last night: Use today's session to set up tomorrow's session, and then quit early today.
5. Start by writing by hand. Move the hand slowly.
6. Go write outside.

Part 3

Your Written Words Take Shape: Declaring Your Book Finished

OR SOME
Physiological Descriptions

Chapter 25

Writing Is Revising

LAUREN, A STUDENT OF MINE, CAME INTO MY OFFICE LAST week with three poems to send off as part of her application to a summer conference. "I revised them like you said, but I think they got worse," Lauren said. She closed her eyes and wrinkled her perfect nose as she set the papers down on my desk. She seemed a little annoyed with me, like I had maybe helped ruin her poetry.

I laughed. "You did new versions," I said.

Lauren looked at me, in that cranky but polite *What now?* way students look at their professors.

"Versions are good," I said.

She frowned harder.

I laughed and nodded. I've been there, too.

No matter how badly we may want it to, revision just doesn't go in a straight line. It's not a process of improvement; it's a process of learning. Revision means you "re-see" your piece. You see it again and again and again, in a slightly different light each time. Some lights are more useful, more flattering, more interesting. Some aren't. Revision is information gathering. It's not a slow and steady always-forward moving march toward perfection (although that is how I first learned it, and how I *used* to teach it: *Let's make it better right now!*).

Revision means making a mess, not straightening up. (*Editing* is straightening up.)

I had to remind Lauren, as I have to remind myself every day: Most of our time as writers is spent revising. *Making versions.* I did an analysis of my own writing this week. Eighty percent of my writing time is spent revising. Not editing/revising, but real revising. Twenty percent is spent on new things, actual editing, straightening up my bookshelves, looking for a stapler that works ...

Writing *is* revising.

There's no way around it.

Writing is rehearsing—going over and over our paragraphs and pages and passages until we get them *close enough to perfect.* Writing is *not* furniture assembly. There are no directions that, if followed in order, will give you a perfect novel. The pieces you create do not come with repair manuals. There are guidelines (make it look like other novels) and principles (drama is interesting, reporting feelings is not). But you basically work without a net. You go to the desk every day, and you put on your skates and give your new idea a whirl.

You work *through* writing. You don't build a piece in some perfect order, step by step, clearly, precisely, done.

Every time I work on a piece, I make some parts better and some parts worse. I add some new parts and leave some parts—the parts I do not know what to do with—alone. I am basically, each day, writing a different *version* of the piece. When I am sick of making versions, I choose the one I think is best, polish it to the best of my ability, and submit it for publication. After a version has been rejected a few times (or a dozen times), I again do a new version of it. Sometimes, I end up choosing an earlier version. Were the later versions a waste of time? Not in my mind. The versions are how I learn. It's like taking a hundred photographs of something in order to get the perfect one.

With each version, I learn more about the truth of the piece, so I know which one to pick, which one is right, even if it is an early draft. Learning is a series of little improvements punctuated by many, many, many terrible disasters.

Look at professional baseball. Hoops. Golf. The Olympics. When athletes practice, what they essentially do is *another version.* Skaters don't get to some point where they never fall. When an ice skater does her routine—it's today's version.

The whole point of doing the version is to learn things. There will be new mistakes that weren't there yesterday. There will be little triumphs, flourishes, changes, maybe some new bobbles. Same music. Same choreography. But each day, the skater handles it a little differently. And she learns something. She probably doesn't ever go to the rink *knowing in advance* what she is going to learn. The version itself teaches her.

We writers have inherited some bizarre notion that when we sit down to work we will *improve the writing*, but it isn't quite that simple.

The skater knows that her practice is all about *getting to know the piece better.*

The little changes you make increase the power of your book. Moving into its deeper levels, carving out more nuance, honing meaning, establishing pattern, intensifying the good parts that you already have. This is the way you make a piece better. The many, many, many little changes.

But how do you know which little changes to make? Maybe you will make your writing worse. And what about all that time? Haven't you sat there in front of your screen moving passages around, back and forth, feeling like you're getting nowhere? You've tinkered with a single sentence *for days.*

That's why revision is called *writing.* This is what you do in your studio during your writing time. Try different things. Make versions. Of sentences, of pieces, of entire paragraphs, of whole novels. Try it one way, then try it another way. Read the two out loud, make a third, incorporating the best of both. Etcetera.

This is what becoming a great writer is all about. Learning your weaknesses and learning your strengths. You try, in each version, to do more of what you know is good (write in scenes, don't use too much dialogue, avoid forced rhymes, use examples) and less of what you know is weak (over-explaining, a character sitting alone with her thoughts). You make new mistakes, things you didn't even know you could *do* wrong, and you correct for those. Writing is a process of attempts and failures and occasional magical got-it-right moments.

Beginning writers usually quit too soon. Just because they wrote *something*, they feel a sense of accomplishment. But you aren't really writing until you're revising, creating new versions. Versions are how you figure out why you did it the way you did, if it should stay that way, and if it can be said better.

Versions give you deeper access to the good writing that often lurks underneath the plain old writing that tends to come out first. *Versions reveal the truth*. It's during the second, third, or fourth time that you get at *what's important* and real. The sequence, the variations that emerge, ultimately reveal the best shape for the piece.

I like to have my students do new versions of their pieces *by hand.* This really works! Don't use your typed copy; put it aside. You create a new version *blind*. Expect much resistance the first time you attempt this. "What?" you may say. "No computer? Are you nuts?"

Just try it.

See what happens.

Time and time again, writers say that all the good stuff comes back up in the new version while the dross falls away. I don't know why it works, but it does. Writing by hand forces you to slow down, and slowing down acts as a kind of compass, aligning you to what's good and real and right and true. Only when you write what's *important to you* can you really get to the truest version, the best incarnation. It's hard to write crap when you're writing by hand; it's easy to spew on a keyboard.

Many writers I work with cling too tightly to the original version. One of the best things about creating versions is it forces you to release your tight death grip on the first draft. It makes you fly free, and that's where the happy accidents, the cool insights, the great new turns of phrase happen. When you are enslaved to the original, you are limited.

The ego wants to be done. It wants to get an A. It doesn't want to revise. The artist—the successful artist—wants to play, wants to wallow in the piece, wander, go off track, marry purple to orange, turn up the volume, introduce lions. Making versions honors both parts of self.

Revision is about seeing more clearly, seeing things you hadn't noticed before. It's essential to the craft of writing, and it's a process devoted to *changing your mind.* That's why revision is so thrilling.

ON YOUR PAGE: *Exercise 27*

Try four versions of a piece you think is fairly successful.

Try four versions of a piece you feel is failing.

This exercise could take several days, or even longer. Choose short pieces while you are training to operate the versions tool, which is a kind of machine, really.

If you are working in a writing group, bring in all the versions and trade with a partner. You are guaranteed to have the kind of discussion that helps you grow as a writer. What does each version do well? What are your weaknesses as a writer? What are some of your bad habits? What are you good at? What do you tend to avoid? What's more interesting in one draft? What is getting lost? Choose your favorites.

Chapter 26

Just Want to Be Done

"I JUST WANT TO BE DONE," JANIS SAID TO ME ON THE PHONE over spring break.

"Oh, no," I said. "Not again."

"No, really. I am just *so done.* I can't look at it anymore."

Janis always says this when she is finished with her working draft and in the middle of her first major revision.

I'm always saying it, too.

It's a total lie. We don't just want to be done. We want to not wreck our books.

Every writer I know reaches this stage. "Just-want-to-be-done-itis" is a nasty little virus that typically strikes during the revision process. It's like a wart. You pick at it. You obsess about it. *I have worked so hard on this book. I have worked harder on this than anything else. I just want to be done. I don't want to work any more.*

What is really happening is a giant fear attack. You wish you were done—that it was good just like it is. You are scared to look at it again deeply, because you are afraid you'll find hideous flaws, horrendous things you have said, idiotic sentences. You are afraid you won't know how to fix these things. You wish you didn't even know about the problem; you kind of close your eyes and tiptoe around.

Of course there's always more work to do on any book, and at some point you have to let it go and call it Good

Enough. But successful writers, published writers, continue to work on their books long after they first hear the "I'm done!" chant.

This is why it's important to understand that you most likely aren't done the first time you start to hear "I'm done." Usually this voice surges up late in the revision process when you're so, so close. It's fear talking. And you have to stay focused.

"Janis," I said, trying to quickly come up with a way to politely keep her from self-imploding.

"No, Heather, I know what you are going to say. I'm just sending it to my agent on Friday—*whatever shape it is in.* That's it. Friday is my deadline."

"No, honey. No. No!" I envisioned myself flying to Texas, rushing to her mailbox, pulling out the manuscript, saving it, saving her, saving us all. "It's not ready."

"How do *you* know?" she said, testily. (Sometimes having a writing partner is exactly like having a spouse.)

I knew because I had just read through her book and suggested changes; she took lots of my ideas and rewrote during two mad, hot weekends while her husband and son went pig hunting in the valley. I knew she needed another read-through, a few weeks to let the book sit, to check over the revisions, make adjustments. This is how a novel is written.

Janis was doing what she always does in the home stretch. She decides she has given enough time to this book. It's better than anything she has written so far. There's a ton of stuff to get caught up on in real life.

We writers want to believe we're unfettered wild geniuses; too brilliant really to fiddle around with details, pagination, spell checking, polishing. We smack down the main scenes.

We have passages of brilliant writing. The plot holds together, basically, and there are some excellent moments in our book. *Isn't that enough? Can't someone else take care of the other stuff?* Tables of contents, indexes, chapter titles, fixing the weaker scenes—*Aren't there people who do that?*

Well, yes. Of course there are.

They're called writers.

That would be you.

Just as no one loves your kids as much as you do, not even the greatest editor on the planet will care as much about your book, its details, its perfection, its publication, its success as you do. *You must be your own editor* before you send the book out of your house and into the world.

Become your dream editor, going through your book *again and again,* reading it with an eye toward perfection and polish. Everything—big and small—that can be improved *you* must improve.

Many writers believe—secretly or openly—that someone else will do this. They want their teachers to do it. "Fix it for me," they say. "I need your comments." They want an agent to do it. "Won't my agent get it ready for publication?" They want that editor who exists in their mind, that fantasy person from yesteryear who is so devoted to their genius and their book that she puts everything on hold to help them fix it.

It just doesn't work that way.

Not every writer passively expects someone else to do part of his work; there are plenty of writers who do everything they can to their books and then some. And after they've set aside their project for a while, they return to it and *do even more to improve the book.* You are competing with these authors.

And this whole "I need someone to help" thing is really a lie—it's a distraction. You have Six Wise Guides. You have a great brain. You have paper. You have a draft. You have everything you need to make your book better. You have put too much work into it to stop now.

When you start hearing the voices—*You should be done. You're done. You need help. You're done!*—and you find yourself saying, "I just want to be done!"—STOP IMMEDIATELY. Quarantine this virus early, before it spreads and convinces you it's right.

Don't send your book out too soon.

Wait.

Stop.

Sit.

It took years to get to this point—three more months aren't going to change the entire course of your publishing career; you aren't missing anything—your focus is inside: in the book and in your head. It is wrong to send it out now. Figure out what you need to do. This is no one else's job but yours.

Come back to the book as an editor, hiring a very sophisticated, brave, experienced part of yourself (we all have that stuff in us, too). Get back to work. You aren't done yet.

When you do send your book out, send it out from one professional to another. Treat agents and editors exactly as you wish to be treated. You wouldn't want them to send you contracts that are *kind of* revised, trusting you to find the weaker parts and fix them up. You wouldn't want your agent to try to sell your book dressed in shorts and a striped T-shirt because she didn't have time to put on a suit—she wanted to *get the big meeting over with so she could go play.* Take your time. Get your manuscript really ready.

Writing this book will take a lot longer than you want it to take. Hasn't everything fabulous in your life taken more time than you thought it would?

Janis ended up sending her book to four agents, all of whom sent it back saying the manuscript still needed some work. She's revising now that it's summer and she's home from teaching for three months.

Did she lose time sending it out too soon?

Maybe. Maybe not.

It doesn't really matter. She had to do it. She got the idea in her head, and the *just want to be done* bugs wouldn't leave her alone. She did what they said. She got "done."

Except she's not.

If you can stop these voices from stopping you (and this is *very* hard to do), you will be able to do deeper work than ever before. Pushing yourself will make you a better writer; you keep setting the bar a little bit higher, training yourself to go places you haven't gone before.

ON YOUR PAGE: *Exercise 28*

Have you had just-want-to-be-done-itis before? Maybe when you painted a room, and you cut corners, literally? Are there times you have rushed the end of a project after putting in so many hours? Has this worked out well, ever? Do you know why you do this? Think about it, or talk about it with a writing friend or your writing group. It can be hard to listen for this stuff—it's very subtle, very deep in your brain, which is why it's so powerful. Then come up with a list of responses to these "I just want to be done" voices. It's best to have a counter-attack prepared in advance.

Chapter 27

Reality Agents

THE WORD "AGENT" IS DERIVED FROM A WORD THAT MEANS *to drive, to lead, to act.* A literary agent "drives" your book around to various publishers, leading it out into the world. She takes action on your behalf, producing contracts and taking meetings and making deals. However, too many writers give up their own power to *drive, lead, act* by thinking, wrongly, that because agents do these things, writers don't have to.

In reality, you do not have to have an agent.

A literary agent, like a real estate agent, can help. A lot. But she doesn't have magic powers—she's not the buyer, she's not the bank, she's not a writer, and she's not a editor. She can't make a flawed book good. She can only take a product—your book—and drive it or lead it as far as its quality allows. Don't give all your power over to agents. Most of the work you can and must do yourself.

I have found publishers for all of my books on my own by introducing myself and my current project to editors at conferences, submitting my manuscript to contests and appropriate publishers (who take unsolicited manuscripts), and studying current publishers' catalogs and finding good matches for my work. I read *Publishers Weekly.* I talk to lots of other writers. For my textbook, I talked to other textbook writers, and my teachers and colleagues, and I learned how to submit book proposals to the right textbook publishers.

My children's book found its home thanks to the illustrator: Amy Young travels to New York every year to show her work to art editors, contacts she has carefully and professionally cultivated for over ten years. I was lucky enough to go along for the ride.

I would *love* to have a big-name agent acting on my behalf, raking in big bucks. But just as a real estate agent can't ask more for your house than the market will bear, a literary agent can't make you into a famous writer unless you write those kind of books. I write poetry and short fiction and children's books. The markets are small. I tried to find an agent while *simultaneously* pursuing publication at smaller presses, where I don't need an agent. (Why share 15 percent of your profits with someone else if you can do the work yourself, *For Sale By Owner*?)

I read books on how to market my own book and manage a literary career. I'm sure I made lots of mistakes and missed opportunities, but I like that when the royalty checks come (for my poetry book this year, the check was for $4!) no one else is taking a cut. If I were writing blockbuster novels, I would definitely have to have an agent. But I am not. I can and should do this work myself.

I met a beautiful writer, Eleanor Blevins, age eighty-two, at a writing conference. She came to me during our one-on-one session prepared to work on her young adult novel about Melvil Dewey, the originator of the Dewey Decimal System. I had read her proposal and sample chapters, and I had notes and comments to share with her. Before we got started, I asked her if she had any burning questions she wanted to be sure we covered during our short session.

Eleanor, in a narrow blue suit of beautiful quality, leaned back in her chair. She flung her palm to her brow. She said, "How do I get an agent! I need an agent!"

Then, she sort of collapsed onto the conference table and put her head down.

"Is your book finished?" I said, after a quiet moment.

"I know it could be better, but I have already queried all these agents," she said.

"Are you willing to work on it more?" I said, thinking we were dealing with a case of just-want-to-be-done-itis.

"I'm not sure what I could do," she said.

I could see a lot Eleanor could do to make her book stronger. A more vivid opening. Tighter scenes. Less summary. She just needed to go through the whole thing again. It wouldn't be hard work—she had a great plot, the book had wonderful bones. I felt like a real estate agent, surveying a grand old house that needed some repairs, but nothing structurally. Updating, really. It would take a few months, I was sure of that. But could Eleanor commit to this process?

"I don't know how to get an agent, and I know I have to have one!" Eleanor covered her ears with her hands.

What didn't she want to hear? An agent wasn't the next step for Eleanor. A rewrite was.

I feared she'd been sort of brainwashed by a session at the writing conference where some writer on the dais told everyone "You have to have an agent." Well, for some kinds of books, yes. It sounds sexy and wonderful; writers love name-dropping agents they've queried or met in passing at a conference. It can feel like you've *made it* when you have an agent, like your work is done—someone else is representing you. Heady.

"I just feel like it's so late." Eleanor put her head back down, and tears came to my eyes. I wanted to help her so badly. I wanted to show her she could take the lead, do the rewrite and the agent *would come.*

This Agent Illusion Syndrome—that you have to have an agent to succeed—happens to a lot of book writers. We get a good start on a book, and maybe after the first draft or maybe even sooner, we get excited and we get sidetracked. We have an overwhelming feeling *we are behind* and *we aren't doing it right* and *we must mind our careers and have an agent or we really shouldn't be trying to write a book*. We feel we really will finish the book better if we go ahead and get an agent—he will help us! We don't want to invest all the hard work in a rewrite if the agent is just going to tell us to do it another way.

At writing conferences there are always a few agents, and they always have lots of energy swirling around them. We see them and think, *Oh, I'm doing it all wrong—who do I think I am, no agent, how can I be a book writer, seriously? Every good one has an agent!*

But it's not true. Agents work for writers. There are some good agents. There are some weak agents. They aren't magical. They aren't rewriting services or life coaches. They're in business. They can sell good books, finished books. That's it. All the action is up to you, the writer.

In the stuffy little hotel conference room, I took Eleanor's cool palm in my hands and said, "It's fine that you sent the book off. It's fine that you don't have an agent yet. I'm going to recommend you do what you already know: Convert the first two introductory chapters into scenes—

exciting scenes. And then send the manuscript to me and two other people, and then do a whole other draft. *Then,* query agents and publishers. And you have to query fifty before you even think about feeling rejected. But we have to get the book so good, so finished, so amazing, first."

"But all that work. I feel like I don't have time. I'm so old!"

I held Eleanor's hand and looked her in the eye, and I reminded her how important her book was, how far she had come, how much the world needed it. She was so close! Why stop now?

Our quest for an agent—it's the child part of the self coming forward and asking Mom to take over from here because we don't think we can do it.

It's good to be conscious of the agent process and good to learn how to write a query and pitch your project. But it isn't good to get completely sidetracked by agents and editors and publishing and advances and your book tour *during the middle of the book-writing process.*

Eleanor felt she was doing everything wrong. She felt everything was taking too long, she felt she lived in the wrong state (Indiana) to be a real writer, she felt too old (she's four-score plus), and she felt wrong, wrong, wrong, and behind, behind, behind, behind. *If only she had an agent all would be well. Someone to watch over her. Someone to guide her. Someone to lead her from page to page, book to book, someone to cheer her on.*

I have had this same exact thing happen to me. The agent thing kicks up a very powerful set of doubts and fears and longings. I doubted I was really a writer, a real writer anyway, because I didn't have an agent. Being agentless in the literary world can make you feel like you are in grubby sneakers at a fancy cocktail party. It can make you feel like an outsider, disconnected from some secret society where all the action is. And maybe you are. But that doesn't have to be a bad thing.

I said gently and quietly to Eleanor that I thought her chapters were really good. Her proposal needed to be rewritten. I asked if she could send me her cover letter, after the manuscript was complete, so we could work on it together. I said again, "Finish the book first. Then we will query agents. This is a great project. You have been writing for years—you know how to write. But finish the book. What will you do when the agent says yes, says to send it immediately? You'll have to rush and you will feel pressure, and we don't write well that way. Finish the book, and then we can worry about the agent queries."

Eleanor took a sip of water.

I could tell it had gone really well.

She pulled herself together and said thank you. And as she stood to leave, she said, "Heather."

"Yes?"

She put her beautiful frail pale hand on the doorknob and turned to me, full on. "I need an agent, I know I do."

When Eleanor got back to her apartment in Indiana, she telephoned me. She was in a full-blown freak-out. This is a woman with a Ph.D., a woman who has published book reviews and academic articles, written a dissertation, and who authors a regular column in her local newspaper. And she was freaking out. "I have a letter from one of the agents I queried," she said.

"That's great! Who?"

She told the story. One of the agents she had contacted about her Melvil Dewey young adult book before even going to the conference loved her idea. He'd read the sample chapters and asked if she could send the—you guessed it—complete manuscript. Right away.

"What do I do now?" Eleanor wailed. "What do I tell them? I am afraid I have ruined everything! I'm so nervous now, I can't write a word!"

Eleanor's quandary is a common one. We know in our hearts the work isn't ready. But we feel rushed, pressured. So we send it out anyway. We want an agent to be interested in us, but when one is—when one actually responds to the *I have a great book here!* messages we send out, we freak.

I told her I have done this, too. This exact same thing. I have gotten nearly done, written a good first draft (of a novel and also of a textbook), and then queried editors and agents, half-sure not one will call me back, half-hoping they all will, and completely hoping the exact right person will *help me finish the book and revise it beautifully.*

We hold in our minds two conflicting notions. On one hand, we believe we will never get published—it's too hard, the odds are too great, our work sucks, we really aren't talented enough, publishing has gone down the tubes because everything is owned by Rupert Murdoch, and no one cares any more. *At the same time* we believe someone will take us on and polish our rough edges and the book's rough edges, too, we will sell millions of copies, and our agent will godparent our children.

So we send out the agent queries. Sure we take *some* of the advice we hear—just enough to make us feel we are in the game. Secretly nurturing dreams of great success, we send off a few sample chapters, secretly nurturing expectations of failure.

And we do this again and again and again.

I made Eleanor a timetable.

We saw on paper what she would have to do to finish the manuscript, to get it ready to send to the agent. It was doable (if she resigned from the garden committee and her condo's complaint board).

Together, we drafted a letter to the agent, explaining the draft would be in the mail on May 1—three months from now. No excuses, no detail, just a clean purchase of three months for Eleanor. Now she had a deadline. She would finish the book, and she would do a conscientious rewrite. And then she would send it.

She learned how afraid she really was (most of us are) of the thing she has dreamed of, book publication. When it came knocking, she hid in the closet. She learned that her book wasn't really finished and that it is a lot easier to wait until the book is as good as it can get before sending out agent queries—even though the entire process is slow and difficult.

Finish your book.

During the writing and full revision process (for most people, this entire takes at least one year, and very often several years) ignore the pressure to get an agent.

Agents broker manuscripts to publishers; they don't run rescue agencies. You are a grown-up now, and you will have to do this *on your own.* As you finish your book and research the agent querying process, also study up on how to be your own agent. This will help you stay in control of the driving, leading, acting. You take on an agent like a pilot takes on a co-pilot.

Give yourself more time than you think you need to finish this book. Really, really, really make it as good as you can get it. I did thirteen versions of my first book of short stories, *Georgia Under Water*, and *then* I got a book contract and an editor. And then we did *four more significant* revisions. During that process, way too early when I was first publishing the stories from that collection in magazines, I started querying agents. And again in the middle, when I thought I should have an agent because my friends were getting them. And again toward the end, when I was sending the book to small presses and contests. I am still looking for an agent. And, meanwhile, publishing books.

When you write, write.

And when you need an editor, call in that most trusted part of yourself.

You don't need an agent until you have a fabulous finished book in hand. And then remember what an agent does and does not do.

You need to be the total master of this project.

You need to own it, literally, wholly for yourself.

ON YOUR PAGE: *Exercise 29*

Pretend you have contacted an agent and she has said, "Your book sounds great! Please send it to me. I'll get back to you within a month." Then give your manuscript *as it is that very day* to a smart, trusted writer friend. Have her write you a letter about why she is or is not going to represent it. Remember, think *sales rep*. Choose a friend who is savvy about the marketplace (if you do not have any of these kinds of friends, you need to sign up for a writing conference!) and encourage her to be as honest as she can be about the book's strengths and weaknesses. What is going to appeal to readers? What is going to give them pause? You do not have to take any of her advice, but this exercise is absolutely essential—a dress rehearsal—before you send your book out into the real world.

Advanced version: If you feel you can afford it, hire a teacher or freelance editor (be sure you do your research, and talk to a few people who have worked with this person; read the person's finished products to make sure she will understand your vision. There are editors-for-hire who are reputable, who can really help you, but you want to take the time to find the right person).

Reminder: Always have your writing group, friends, or teachers look over your agent query letter and your book proposal (if that applies), and make sure all your envelopes and stamps and printer ribbons are *perfect*.

Chapter 28

Not Too Old, Not Too Late

ACCORDING TO DAVID GALENSON, PH.D., AUTHOR OF Old Masters, Young Geniuses: The Two Life Cycles of Artistic Creativity, most artistic types peak later in life. "While early breakthroughs get the attention, lots of creative people—writers, painters, chefs—learn as they go, using trial and error," he says. And he's right. My older students are usually more prepared, more able to establish a daily writing habit, and more capable of insightful, rich writing.

Writing takes a long time to learn how to do. One of my teachers in graduate school said the average writing apprenticeship—the time it takes to learn how to write fairly well on your own and sell your work—is ten years.

I teach college students at a very traditional college where first-year students are eighteen years old, sophomores are nineteen, etc., and to a person, they feel *too young* to be taken seriously. They feel underprepared, dumb, not well read, and inferior. They are intimidated by other writers, success, and fame. They feel incredibly behind and overwhelmed by all the reading they have to do, all the work it's going to take. They wish they were older. Wiser. Not living in a dorm. *What real writer lives in a dorm?* One of my students, Nicole, wrote, "My age is a burden sometimes. I feel I'm not experienced enough to write about certain things. I do not know what I am doing. I don't know how to portray experiences to the reader."

My younger students, unlike my middle-age pupils, are more likely to binge write—working intensely for ten or fifteen or even thirty hours at a stretch, achieving breakthrough after breakthrough. (Middle-aged people tend to fall asleep after about twelve hours of *anything.*) Younger writers take more risks, reveal more, play with language, fool around on the page, worry less about sounding stiff or formal or grammatical; they'll make a giant mess and figure it all out later.

On the other hand, many of the students I work with at conferences and workshops are in their forties, fifties, or sixties. They feel too old. They feel constricted in their writing dreams—if only they were younger and had more time, they would be able to follow their passions and really *do* it. "I don't know how to write from the point of view of a twenty-year-old," Terry, one of my summer program students, told me. She's an accomplished journalist in her late forties. "I don't know what I'm doing. It's too late to start a new career."

Everyone thinks they're the wrong age. *Everyone* thinks they're starting to write their books at the wrong time.

There is no wrong time.

You should start now. *Today*, if you haven't already. If you have started, your timing is extraordinary.

Writers—all writers, at all ages and all stages—must realize all they have is the *now.* Just this moment. There's not another "time" that's better for you to write. A certain age when it's all going to click. You haven't missed anything, and you haven't started too early or too late.

Art is one of the few things (unlike sports, becoming a mother, making a career in business, applying for social security) that is completely, wholly blind to age and time and birthdays. The muse just doesn't care about your age.

If you're eighty years old, you can spend the next five years writing and accomplish more at age eighty-five than many writers do in a lifetime.

Don't use age as an excuse for not giving your writing 100 percent of your attention and energy. You are the exact perfect age. If you're fifteen years old and reading this book, you're fully authorized to begin a serious writing life—lots of people start writing at fifteen, younger than fifteen. There's no reason why you can't be the youngest person at writing conferences, the youngest person to write a great novel, the youngest person to spend late nights writing, writing, writing. Your age is irrelevant.

If you're forty or fifty or sixty and reading this book, stop worrying about your age and why you didn't start earlier. You've lived a little. You know how to stop unproductive mind patterns. When a distracting thought comes up, recognize it for what it is and banish it from your mindscape. You have accomplished (or not) some of the other things on your life to-do list, and *now is the time.*

The perfect time.

Your age gives you perspective. When you're middle-aged, it's easier to be patient with your mistakes. You've read more. You probably have a little bit more money than when you were sixteen, so you can subscribe to some journals, buy Wise Guides, afford reams of paper. Starting a writing life when you're sixty is quite brilliant and many people do it. Jimmy Carter and his wife started writing books in retirement; so do many others.

Remember, when you were little you wanted to be big. Now that you are big, you want to be little. That's all illusions, distractions, useless information to you, the writer, the artist.

Embrace the exact age you are and stop thinking in "should haves."

Art is timeless.

So are you.

ON YOUR PAGE: *Exercise 30*

Get the Big Picture clear for yourself. Cast your mind forward ten years. It doesn't matter how old you are now. What do you want to accomplish as a writer these next ten years? Do you write books quickly or slowly? Some writers can finish a book in one year. Others require five years to create and complete one novel. What kind of writer are you? Map your writing life in terms of decades, focusing on the future, not the past.

Chapter 29

Dress Rehearsal: Attending a Writers Conference

WRITING IS A SOLITARY PRACTICE, SO WRITERS NEED TO GET experience at being out in the world and talking to professionals. This means that before you send out your work, send out yourself: Go to a writing conference.

Even if you mix it up with seasoned professionals working at the top of their game in your normal day job, you still need to practice interacting with the pros of the writing business. Let's face it, writers can just get so *weird.* It's all the time we spend alone; it's a job hazard. We can get socially isolated and strange: prickly, out of touch, easily irritated. We can lose our social finesse ... if we ever had much to begin with. We miss a lot of popular culture, because we don't have time to watch gobs of television or read magazines; we have precious writing hours to get in each day, and after about a year of a daily commitment to writing, we might notice we've grown just a little bit peculiar. Talking out loud in the car more. Beauty regimen gone (and it was pretty bare-bones to begin with).

You have to say no to many fun outings if you're going to finish your book; a conference is your chance to practice being social in the writing-world context. In addition to networking, learning, finding amazing books at the book fair, meeting new people, and having lots of fun in the bar at night, a writing conference hones the parts of yourself you need to use to sell and market your book.

Don't be weird. No strange costumes. No needy behavior. No gimmicks. Don't try too hard. Don't impose yourself or your manuscript on others. Don't hoard the invited guests and speakers, don't monopolize, don't cling to the wall. There's something about writers in a pack that brings out the scary parts of human nature. There's a kind of desperation. People act like this is their one and only chance to get published. They get rude and, well, just plain weird. Relax. Be normal. You're just here to learn some things and practice talking about your writing to strangers. That's basically the public life of a writer.

You're not going to this conference to be discovered. Nor to hand out your six-hundred-page novel about baby pigs to everyone you meet, nor to sell your self-illuminating bookends, nor to collect autographs. Learn. Practice. Learn. Practice.

Choosing the right conference and having a good experience requires four things on your part: Preparation. Discovery. Connection. Practice. (The same things required to write a book.)

Preparation

First, research the potential writing conferences that interest you. You can do this online at places like www.WritersDigest.com and www.shawguides.com. Send for brochures from conferences that feature writers you like or that are close to where you live. Universities and community colleges often have conferences in the summer; check out the ones at the major universities in Iowa, Nebraska,

Vermont, and North Carolina. Ask teachers and other writers for recommendations.

When you've decided where to go, make sure you're properly prepared to attend. You need a clear agenda—a conference strategy. This strategy has to be founded on realistic expectations. You probably won't have an agent say, "Sign this contract—I have to represent you. This is fantastic work!" Although it has happened, it's extremely rare (see Chapter 26: Just Want to Be Done). You need a practical agenda, one you can really control. You need some very specific, attainable goals so you will know whether the conference has been useful.

Make a list of what you want to accomplish and carry it at all times to refer to if you feel a little lost or overwhelmed. A writing conference can be intense, depressing, exhilarating, crazy, life altering, mildly helpful, or a series of tiny blunders. If you go prepared, you'll return to your book project with new energy, a greater sense of purpose, and professional focus.

Here's one writer's list of goals for the Whidbey Island Writers Conference—a healthy mixture of four days of workshops, seminars, small group meetings, and large discussions with panels of agents and editors.

1. Come home with e-mail addresses for ten writers (at about my level) with whom I can exchange work.
2. Make myself talk to at least two famous authors—without feeling like a total fool.
3. Attend at least one morning session and one afternoon session each day.

4. Write each morning, if only for ten minutes.
5. Be prepared with a perfectly practiced pitch so I do well at the pitch session (if I get one).
6. Ask questions of Miss Editor at XYZ Press about the house's apparent new direction—how has being bought changed their philosophy?

Don't ask a question that could be easily answered through preparation; the agent or editor will feel like she is wasting her time. Reach for superb questions, ones that are general enough to be appropriate for a conference conversation but specific enough that you leave with something you can really apply to your book, book proposal, or writing life. Preparation involves taking a few hours to write down perhaps as many as a hundred questions and then narrowing your list down to the ten you want answered by the end of the conference weekend.

Discovery

Next in your conference journey is the discovery stage. You're going to writing school! Take notebooks and pens. You're there not to be discovered, but in order *to discover.* At the conferences, you'll listen—for a day or more—to many writers, and you'll learn *a lot* about how to prepare your manuscript, how to write a novel, how to do dialogue, what trends are hot, how these people talk and behave. Some of it is overt—take notes at a session. A lot of it is subtle—the conversation you overhear in the hallway, the attitudes of the editors—what they say *between the lines* of their talks. You're absorbing all this writing-world stuff to polish you as a writer. It's all going to be helpful later.

When you're at the conference, pay attention to *little discoveries* that lead to better questions. You're "on" the whole time. You're working to notice subtle things and make new connections.

Connect with people who are taking notes. Connect with the serious writers. Don't let fear and anxiety attract you to the Bad Boys or Wallflowers. Risk being a little bit dorky. "Hi, that was a *great* question you asked at the Pitch Perfect session. I'm looking for a few writing partners. Want to trade e-mails with me and my new friend, Harold? We are also writing literary romances."

I have noticed there are two kinds of people at conferences: people with clear agendas and people who like the *idea of writing*. The focused participants are social, appropriate, not nervous, and articulate. This is work; it doesn't come naturally to most writing personalities, at least not in my experience. The people in the other group like being around writers and books and publishing. They like the idea of meeting agents and editors. These attendees may not actually write, and they aren't at the conference to work. They're there to be spectators. They want to write ... *someday*.

There is nothing wrong with being one of the fun amateur wannabes, just checking out the scene. You don't have to be a writer to get something out of a writing conference. When I go to a triathlon, I'm not there to win. I'm not very fast or very sure of myself. I have no idea how to enter into technical discussions. I don't like that they write on my skin with a marker; I'm not very triathlete-ish. I wander in a daze, overwhelmed, but I love being around all those athletes! I gawk at their fancy bikes and eavesdrop on their sexy conversations, which always contain *numbers* in them. Spectator-participants, like me, are a complaint of some super-serious triathletes. But our entry fees, our manpower, our energy, our enthusiasm—*we* create the platform for the cool kids. We are the backbone of the sport.

If you are just starting out in your writing career, it's fine to wander around with no plan, to get excited about famous people, to waft in and out of sessions, to sleep late and party with the writers in the hot tub way after it is officially closed. A lot of writers look to the conference to inspire them to write.

Connection

You go to the conference to connect with new writing mates, people like you, people to trade with over e-mail. Not agents or editors, unless your book is perfect (which it probably isn't). In order to come home with ten names (your minimum goal), you'll probably need to ask twenty people. It's like dating. You'll be turned down flat. It doesn't matter. Keep asking until you have ten numbers/e-mail addresses. It's good practice for the writing life; rejection is part of the deal.

Bring home ten names, because only two or three of those people will be able to give their work *and* your work the time both deserve. One address won't do. Two of your names won't be as committed to this process as they say they are. Three others will mean well and intend to trade with you, but I have found again and again that less than 30 percent of conference attendees are as serious as you and I are. That said, many writers (myself included) have found terrific writing partners by going to writing conferences and making a concentrated effort to connect *with other writers.*

Agents *do* find new writers at conferences. But overwhelmingly, authors make getting an agent their only agenda. I wouldn't do that. I use the conference for other purposes. I mostly want to improve as a writer. I always will.

Practice

The last phase of your conference plan is practice. Practice good probing conversational questions. Practice being a little bit nerdier, a little more inquisitive, a little more outgoing, more normal, less weird. Practice being confident. It's usually just a minor adjustment, not a whole personality overhaul.

If you haven't been to lots of writing conferences or talked with tons of editors and agents, it's normal to be nervous, to talk too much, to state the obvious, to have unrealistic expectations. Your new job is to *practice being a writer.*

The first few times you describe your work to strangers it will be very awkward and strange. Be patient with yourself. You have lived alone with this work for so long! You and the book have been locked away in a secret room, just the two of you. Shining the harsh light of conversation on something as private and fragile as a book manuscript can feel invasive. Notice what other people say to make their work sound good. What makes you want to know more, what has you watching for their books to come out in the bookstore? Do less of what makes you blush and cave in.

A writing conference stretches you. It gets you ready for the interactions that will mark your writing life—meetings with your own editor, her boss, her boss's boss. It gets you ready for talking on the phone to the agents who answer your queries down the road. A conference gets you ready for prime time.

A conference is a wonderful workshop for *you, the writer.* You have some typos to you. You may even have a few missing pages (I do!).

Add a new chapter: Conference You.

ON YOUR PAGE: *Exercise 31*

Research writing conferences. Ask friends about the ones they are familiar with. Go to your library and peruse a guide to writing conferences and retreats. Check out the Web sites of three or four conferences. There are conferences for detective writers, children's book writers, romance writers, literary writers, super-advanced poets, general new writers, just-beginning-to-publish writers. What kind of conference looks good to you? What do you want to discover by going? What are you hoping will happen? What do you need to prepare?

Chapter 30

Angus and the Weight Lifted

IN ORDER TO PUBLISH A BOOK, YOU HAVE TO WORK VERY hard, for a very long time, with no guarantees. Some days you believe your book is super fine. Other days you know it's crap. Most days you don't know *how* it's going, and that can be confusing. Never do you know for sure *this book will be published* or *this book is good*. That's a lot of not knowing. Years of it, usually.

Angus had already been through this process of not knowing twice, but it was worth it. He published two successful books with small presses, both of which went to paperback and sold quite nicely. Then Angus began a memoir about being the father of a teenage daughter. His agent loved the idea. Angus worked on the book every day, while teaching full time (including summer) and editing a literary magazine, plus traveling around to promote the first two books. The manuscript grew to several hundred pages, and then it hit five hundred. Angus revised, made the tome shorter, and again, it grew, passing five hundred pages. He worked on the project for three years, starting when his daughter was thirteen and growing distant, and ending when she was sixteen and hardly speaking to him at all.

When he finally felt it was finished, Angus drove himself to New York City to meet with his agent, who'd read the final draft, as well as all the drafts along the way. She had always been encouraging. Angus was excited to hear her strategy for selling the book. As he drove along the parkway, he wondered which publishing houses she would send it to first. He even thought, *Maybe this book would win an award. No one writes about fathers and daughters, not really.* He treated himself to a nice lunch and made his way into the city.

He could tell by the look on her face when he walked into the glass office that it was going to be a difficult meeting. But the news was much worse than he thought. He knew the book was long. The process had been difficult. He knew the topic wasn't super sexy, and his writing wasn't like best-seller writing; this was no *DaVinci Code.*

When his agent spoke, her first words cut through Angus like a sword. "I think you should turn this into a three-page essay," she said. "I love the book, but I can't sell it. You really could get a kick-ass piece out of this, though." She shook her head. She didn't apologize. "I think it's time to move on," she said.

Angus was furious. He felt like crying and throwing his satchel at the glass windows overlooking the city. He begged for a while, he defended the book, he took his carefully written proposal from three years ago and sort of waved it around, rambling about the powerful bonds, the underserved topic, the tricky nature of fathers and daughters, the new material since she'd quit cheerleading.

Angus drove out of the city. The whole meeting had taken only twenty-three minutes. Three years of work, down the toilet in twenty-three minutes—or in three seconds if he only counted the important sentence: "I can't sell it." *Less than three seconds.*

Dazed, Angus wound his way through the familiar freeways and thoroughfares, and by the time he got to New Jersey he was feeling lighter. He felt as if he had left something behind.

In a good way.

By the time he hit Palisades Parkway, heading toward home, Angus was feeling twelve pounds lighter and almost … dare he say … happy.

He could hardly believe it.

He tried to weep.

He tried to call his wife again on the cell phone to ask for pity and understanding and a bourbon, ready and waiting.

But he couldn't get through. Not to his wife. Nor could he get through to the feelings he was expecting to wash over him. The terrible feelings of rejection and despair—where were they? He was expecting to sob or scream. He kept thinking, *It's going to hit me. I'll have to pull the car over.* But Angus, sticking carefully to the speed limit, was stunned, shocked even, to find himself absolutely relieved to be done with that book!

He was not angry.

Relief trumped bummed out, a thousand fold.

He wanted to feel wretched and sorry for himself. He wanted to want to save the book—all those hours! All that paper! All those #78 printer cartridges at $39.98 a pop. But he was thrilled! He sang out loud, "I am a free man!" He was the happiest he had been in, well, three years, since his daughter quit talking to him, got a boyfriend, and closed the door to her room.

Since he had started the book.

The very next day, a Friday, Angus woke up, ever so vaguely hungover, but not really, and sat at his desk. In the gray morning light, he wrote the entire book over in 783 words.

He took all the files and the drafts and manuscript pages and put them in a giant trunk in the basement, and then he put the rocking chair and the old bath mats on top of the trunk. He felt not one iota of loss or regret, which completely shocked him and still does to this day.

It was like the end of a bad marriage. He knew he had been unhappy, but he thought it was *his* fault. After awhile, it just seemed normal.

The three-page version of the five-hundred-page three-year memoir was published in a major magazine, just several weeks after being written.

The Monday after his agent freed him from the Beast, Angus began a new book—a collection of essays about war, and being in college during the Vietnam war, and a whole bunch of other stuff. He wrote the essays in one year and published all but two in fine magazines. Just yesterday he sold the book to a wonderful university press as part of a series of literary nonfiction.

Whenever he gives a public reading, Angus reads the five-hundred-page-memoir-in-three-pages essay. Sometimes he tells the story.

What he doesn't tell is that his daughter is talking to him again. Last weekend they went to a Dada art show—her pick—together.

And he started a new book, writing every day. It's not about her.

Lighten your load. Loosen your grip on your Big Project. Try something radically different; really change how you think about your book and your relationship to your book.

What happened to Angus would knock a lot of writers for a loop. Many would spend months or years querying new agents; carrying a grudge; working on the father-daughter tome; sinking more and more time, effort, money, energy, and printer cartridges into the project.

Shock yourself.

What happened to Angus was an incredible stroke of luck, but it's something we can all emulate, taking his luck and making it our lesson.

Sometimes, the books we're working on just don't get enough of our attention. We think about writing more than we write; we quit when the going gets tough (and it always will). But once in a while, we overwork, overcook, overestimate. Becoming a writer is learning to tell the difference. Have you worked hard enough? Or is this thing just *not going to work*? It's an art, learning the difference.

Angus chose an agent he trusted. He wasn't very happy with her, and he didn't send a thank-you note after she killed the tome. He can't even think about the three years, all the work—he just doesn't even let his mind go there. But she's the same agent who sold his next book in a matter of months, and she's the same agent who's excited about the first seven pages of his current project. Angus is staying the course. (Except when he's not.)

Ever since that weight was lifted off of him, he has felt clearer, more focused—like he's a better writer.

Another thing: Even before his agent said to him, "Angus, this isn't working, and it isn't going to work," Angus had experienced that nagging voice in his head, the one that says *you are faking this, it isn't right.* He ignored that voice for years because he didn't want to believe it. We have to learn, as writers, when the voice is doubt, when it's fear, and when it's bullshit. And we have to distinguish truth—if you listen carefully and bravely and honestly, you will know. With all things, listening to these voices and making fine distinctions takes practice.

We are always learning. As long as we are writing, we are learning, and we are improving our craft. Not every project is successfully published, but that doesn't mean we didn't have to do that project, that we didn't learn something valuable from that project.

Angus had to write his way through that book—he couldn't go around it. He couldn't skip it. The book was a key stage in his writing career; it's a dark stage, and we all have them. Every one of us.

Are you in a light stage right now, writing a book that delights you, something agent-friendly, something that has ease and excitement, groundedness, and stars? Or are you in a dark stage, sticking with a difficult project, a magnum opus, a big old thing you've been carrying around for years? How will you tell the difference between the hard work of writing and dead weight?

Both sit on our shoulders in pretty much the same way.

Ask three readers for their opinion: "Do I stay with this, or do I let it go?" and you will get three different answers. Deciding to give up on a book into which you've invested an enormous amount of time is never easy (but you might be surprised at how much energy you roll over into the next project). It really is like giving up on a marriage. It rarely feels 100 percent absolutely right. You can stay with it and make the best of the bad parts. Or you can settle and try to find agents and editors who can live with the flaws. Or you can also say, "You know what? It's not going to work. I have to move on."

I know I've been encouraging you to stick with your manuscript for eons longer than you ever thought would be necessary and to really give yourself over to this writing life. But, there comes a time, as even very successful book authors know, when you'll write a dud. You'll probably only rarely know *for certain* you're doing the right thing. Confusion is just part of the writing life. Do your best work, and when it isn't Good Enough, try again. Same manuscript, new manuscript? Only you can know.

You do have a fabulous book in you.

Maybe it's time to let it out into the light.

ON YOUR PAGE: *Exercise 32*

Do you have a Giant Book Project that has been dogging you for years? A book you feel you want to write, must write, should write, are writing, will write? What would your writing life be like if you *didn't have this project*? What if someone told you to forget about it? How would you feel? Devastated? Free? A little of both? For today's writing assignment, pretend you have just been told your work of the last three, five, or ten years is not going to be accepted by your agent—she refuses to take the project. Instead of falling into a pit of regret and anger and shame, pretend you decide to be Angus-like, and you feel instead—to your surprise—lightness, happiness, freedom, like you have permission to start fresh. Go ahead and write your entire book in the form of a three-page piece—you are not allowed one word more than 783. Give yourself no more than two hours to complete this assignment.

Then pretend you start a new book—what is it?

Chapter 31

In Pursuit of Publication, Rejection

When my face-blind memoir was featured on national television, my writing friends said, "Publish it now! You have to strike now! It's hot!" *Were they right?* I suddenly felt worried. Panicked. *Was I supposed to do something to maximize the attention, this once-in-a-lifetime exposure? Was I wasting my fifteen minutes of fame?* I wrote to a few agents who had already seen the manuscript, and each one wrote back and said, "Just worry about making the book better." They were absolutely right. The fact that the memoir was featured on television didn't improve the quality of the manuscript. No alchemy happened under the hot lights that turned a weak chapter into a strong one. It would have been great if the book was as polished as it could be *before* the national news came knocking on my door. But it wasn't.

Sometimes we rush to send something off—to an editor, to an agent, to a magazine—before it's ready. Other times we worry a piece to death, revising and revising, making it worse, getting lost, losing years of time—and we're long past the point where it was viable or market-ready.

In this maddening, intoxicating pursuit of publication, it's easy to get distracted—to obsess about timing, to want to be done so badly, to overanalyze obscure messages in rejection slips. The main thing to concentrate on is writing every day so you generate enough momentum, enough energy, to write a complete and polished book.

Publishing and writing are two wholly separate endeavors. It's wrong to house these two businesses in the same room—like simultaneously running a child-care facility and a lion-taming school from your home.

Publication isn't meaningful in and of itself. *Writing is meaningful.* Your work deserves your best energy. It's essential to have separate physical and mental spaces for *writing* and *publishing.* And it's just as vital to recognize that publishing your work involves getting your work rejected. It's a process, not a drama. Rejection is, after all, simply *mail.*

My first book was rejected by ninety agents and fourteen publishers before being accepted by Sarabande Books sans agent; it went on to be a bestseller for them, winning a major prize. In the meantime, I kept writing.

You have to figure out how to deal with rejection like a practical business owner, not a kid with hurt feelings. You must be writing your next book *while the first one is being rejected.* You're going to be asked, "What are you working on now?" *Um, nothing.* Publishers hire writers more than they buy books.

You must carry on, brilliant creative soul! And you can!

Don't let rejection hijack your process—you won't get your work done unless you change your thinking. You have mail coming into your mailbox. A letter. A note saying, "We aren't taking this piece." This note has *nothing to do with your writing life*. That's entirely separate. The rejection note means only one thing: You're a writer engaging in the publication process. This is good! This is a great, celebratory thing!

I've have worked on several magazines, so I know firsthand that a lot of good work is rejected not because it's flawed, but because the editors can only take twenty-two poems out of the thousand they received. Many of them had to go back. Many, many, many, many.

Knowing that this is how the process works helps me keep rejection in perspective, to remember that it's simply mail. It's such a minuscule part of my life. Letters sent back and forth. "Do you want my manuscript?" "No thanks." Okay. New letter, new magazine. *No thanks? No problem.* There are hundreds of magazines. The only thing that really matters is that you keep writing, keep improving your craft. That's the business that *really* matters.

Today I got a rejection from the *Raritan Review*. A full sheet of paper that said, "We read this with interest." Since it was an official letter, I celebrated with a glass of wine. I'm pleased that a person read my work, and the world feels like a better place to me tonight. I am not rejected. I am *read.*

Writer rejection is pretty gentle: It's just a piece of mail. It isn't really about you: it's writer communication. Use rejection to grow stronger, to gain perceptive and become more focused as a writer. Smart writers use rejection to stay tethered to their work. Revise your work any time you feel like it. You don't have to give power to these decision makers—after all, editors are just *readers.* You don't like everything you read. Why must they?

Rejection is absolutely and wholly a part of the writing life. You know how small businesses have customers? And sometimes these customers come in but they don't buy anything in the store? You wouldn't write these customers letters asking for their rationale—"Why didn't you buy anything in my store?" You wouldn't have time for that. You're running a business. Rejection is just a part of the writing business. The more you write, the more you send out, the bigger your playing field, the more rejections you will receive. It's okay to enjoy rejection notices, to save them and celebrate them and share them with other writers. If your work is being rejected, it's a sign you are writing—the most important thing of all.

Rejected writers are *writers.* It's a very public sign that you are reading magazines and researching markets. You're part of the conversation. You're getting your work done. Rejected, and you're in the game.

ON YOUR PAGE: *Exercise 33*

Finish your work, and then mail your manuscript to yourself. Go through all the trouble for nothing. The SASE (self-addressed, stamped envelope), the perfect cover letter (address it to the editor of the magazine or publishing house you are hoping will take your work), the whole enchilada. Go through all the motions perfectly. If you do not have the energy to do this, try to find out why.

Most of the work you send out will come right back. For me, it's 90 percent (I've tracked my submissions carefully for more than twenty years). You have to get used to *giving it away* like this. This exercise helps you develop the proper lightness of touch combined with absolute perfect attention to detail. Do it!

When the work comes, wait until you have a free hour. Sit with the mailing. Take notes. Before you even open it, what impression does the envelope make? Handwritten or typed out? Crazy or clean? Slowly work through every feature of the packet, and be as objective as you can. This is a terrific way to jump-start a stalled project. Chances are you'll have a few very clear revision assignments—and nothing makes for easier writing days than a clear sense of what to do next.

ON YOUR PAGE: *Exercise 34*

Write an acceptance letter to rejection. Explore rejection. What are the other times have you been rejected? Getting it down in writing helps to take the load off of that little slip of paper that comes in the mail, *Sorry.* Often the fact that your work wasn't chosen for a magazine triggers your whole history of rejections (Joey and the prom of '82, that guy on the beach in junior high). Get all that out now.

Put it in perspective. Where does the rejection of your writing fit in the global constellation of Rejection for you? How big of a deal is it in terms of what's going on in the larger world? This is not a guilt trip, just a reality check.

Chapter 32

No One Tells You

When your first book comes out in print, it's hard to be prepared; it's a completely new experience. Mostly, it's fabulous. There's a tangible reward—the book, between its beautiful covers—that you can hold and pet whenever you want. There's attention—telephone calls, e-mails, reviews, maybe radio or television spots—which are all very fun. And there's a lot of good learning and growth in navigating these new experiences. People read your book and tell you how it changed them or made them laugh. The feeling that comes from connecting with another human being is powerful; it feeds you like a really healthy high. You might get to travel around, teach classes, present at schools or to groups of citizens; (some) people listen to you (a little). You have a reason to buy a new outfit. Best of all, you are *done with the book.* You worked hard, and it paid off. You wrote a book. You have proof. No one can take that away from you, ever.

I wish, though, that someone had prepared me for the more difficult things that come with publishing a book.

I didn't need help preparing for fame and fortune; there wasn't much of either really. I didn't need assistance for the onslaught of media attention; no fans trolled past my house, no long lines at bookstores. There were no carpal tunnel issues from book signings. These things—what our culture tells us being published is all about—didn't happen. (If all those things happen to you, you deserve that success; you'll know *exactly* how to cope. You'll do fabulously well.)

No one tells you what *won't* happen.

For most books, their arrival is accompanied by a cheerful but very empty silence.

The book comes out. It's in your local bookstores (because you called and requested that the bookstore manager order a few copies, and you offered to do signings for free). You haven't seen any reviews yet, but you know the book is in the publisher's catalog, and you have six gleaming copies on your coffee table.

But it's so ... very ... quiet.

You've worked so hard, for so long. Your advance was probably less than you thought it would be, and you have to sell books to earn back that advance. When the book comes out, you're excited, expectant, and ready for your life to change but, for the most part, it doesn't.

It's embarrassing for me to admit this, but that's what *I* was expecting when my first book came out. I'd worked so long. It had been rejected so many times. Finally, it found a great home with people who loved it like I loved it. Ta-da! We're here!

Thump.

Very, very quiet.

Very quiet.

I thought when my book came out my *neighbors* would buy it and read it. I thought cousins would buy it and read it and send me chatty long letters. I thought my students would read it, and former boyfriends would write to me, apologizing for being so hasty in their judgments, forgiving all my flaws. Somewhere deep in the recesses of my little brain, I thought my former teachers (especially the freshman composition instructor who gave me a D+ on my first submission to her class) would retroactively raise my grades.

I'm afraid I thought being a published author would be transforming. A Friendly Author version of me, waving down at passersby, the helpful someone everyone knows. This childhood concept of published author stuck with me, and, without my knowing it, still existed when my book came out.

There are some authors—Danielle Steel, Stephen King, Anne Tyler—who are widely read, whose names are household commodities, who have fans drive by their homes and point. Most of us writing and publishing books aren't in that fancy neighborhood, though. The shiny one on the hill, the one with the deep pockets and wide lawn and mysterious gated entry.

Most published authors are in the average neighborhood on the other side of town, the one with the plainer houses, the one that's hardworking, takes its community service seriously. There's no gated entry. We have nice lawns, but we forget to water them sometimes.

Writing a book doesn't gain you entry into the Special Club of Famous Authors. Your life, post-book, looks like your life now.

You devote vast amounts of time (unpaid) to this endeavor, change your whole life around, and work really hard. The people around you sacrifice, and you *still* aren't in the club yet. I think most people don't think it through. If they did, would they still write books?

To be perfectly honest, if I knew how long it would take to write a book, how much work it would be to learn the basic elements of craft, how much more work it would be to learn the business side (which, like most people, I assumed I already knew—ha!), I'm not sure I would have chosen this path. It's a lot harder than I thought it would be, and that scares me to admit. Some days I feel like the quiet surrounding my book is proof that I shouldn't have bothered in the first place.

You might feel this way, too, but you have to keep going. We have to keep going, because without a writing life, who would we be? I would be an empty husk of a person, a cracked bowl.

When you're into book writing and your whole life consists of reading, writing, and publishing, you get a skewed world view. You start to think (or at least I did) that everyone is as interested in books as you are. Television and newspapers report big advances, big print runs, big author news.

Reality check: The club of people interested in books and authors is pretty small. That's why most of your co-workers and friends can tell you who won the last *American Idol*, but they don't know who won the last National Book Award. To us writing can seem like the entire world, because we spend so much of our time in books and around them and under their spell.

I really believed that people would treat me differently—*Look! It's an author!*—after I got published, because *I* am always gaga when I'm around authors. I worship the ground they walk on. I want to know what their lives are like. I buy books containing nothing but photographs of writers' desks, writers' studios, writers' journals, interviews with writers. I want to know what they eat, how they spend their time.

A lot of new authors are surprised after the book comes

out at how fast it's all *over.* It's like Christmas. You wait all year and then poof, the day comes and goes so quickly. The season is over. It's New Year's, and then spring, summer. You are forgotten.

When I published my first book, I thought I would feel different than I did pre-publication. That it would somehow be like losing one's virginity. Like I'd be all special and grown up now.

No one told me. You stay the same.

No one tells you that there is roughly a four-month window where your new book is of interest to someone other than your closest friends. These four months are exciting, and you should plan to make time to be available for readings, lectures, workshops, and interviews. You should also plan to set up these events yourself unless you're hiring a publicity rep to do this for you. This kind of basic publicity is not, as is commonly thought, the job or obligation of the publisher, your editor, or their publicity team. It's your book. It's your job.

No one tells you about author etiquette; hopefully you have good instincts or you know how to find out. Write thank-you notes to every bookstore that hosts a reading and to anyone who invites you to do anything. Show your appreciation to bookstore managers and buyers. Your editor. The salespeople who sell your book. Anyone who helps your book in any way, big or small. They are colleagues, not servants. You are an author, not a royal. (A royal you-know-what.) You are grateful to be published, not "Well, *finally*." You are thinking about your next book. Write back to fans who write you. Thank every one all the time.

No one tells you it's worth paying a professional to get a good author photo and also that some poses are stupid.

No one tells you that while many people may buy your book, not all of them will actually read it. Close friends won't read it. Some close friends will say they have read it, but they haven't read it. No one tells you how to politely make them feel as though you really believe they did read it—even if you suspect they didn't—and you are grateful to them.

No one tells you that being published does not mean you are done learning how to write better. It only means you are getting better. You'll still need to ask for help and guidance. Pay attention to what you still need to learn. Stay curious. Help new writers.

No one tells you to have a good start on your next book project by the time your first book comes out. It's hard to stay focused during the months right before your book comes out when you have the greatest chance of capturing media and bookstore attention. If you already have a job, now you have three: marketing your book, your day job, *plus* your daily writing hours. You must not, no matter what, give up those hours.

No one tells you that you will probably not notice a difference in your bank account. Those who do write and get paid well for it usually deserve it—writing anything takes long, long hours. Writing the specific types of books that earn big advances takes laser-like focus, an extreme commitment to steadiness, discipline, and a deep understanding of market conventions learned only through serious study of those books. Most of us write for very little financial compensation whatsoever.

No one tells you how to market your book. Read books on this topic. Be able to sum up your book in one good sentence. Plan to spend several weeks creating and perfecting this one sentence. Once in awhile, curious, well-meaning, polite, or just good people will ask you, "What is your book about?" You will never be able to come up with something brief and effective and smart on the spot. (If you ever do, write it down!). Most people don't want to know *a lot* about your book. They're asking to *be introduced to it,* to shake hands. Your sentence is that handshake. Then shut up, unless these wonderful curious people ask for more information. Have that paragraph about your book memorized, short, ready.

No one tells you that to get your book to take off, you might have to work really hard, putting in a lot of your own time and money. One writer, a famous self-help book guru, bought ten thousand copies of his first book and drove around to bookstores and handed them out for free, telling a little bit about his approach as he placed the book in the palms of dubious shopkeepers. He's now a multi-millionaire and the author of a series of best-selling guides to making money and being happy.

No one tells you there might be bookstore events held in your honor to which no one comes. If you have been going to the readings and signings of other authors, you can expect to have people come to yours. If you haven't been working on your literary citizenship, your turnout might not be great. I have given readings to one person. I have gone to many places where not one person came, just the bookstore manager (thanks, Cliff!). I have taken the four people who were there out to dinner instead of reading to them (we were all relieved). Every writer I know tells this same story. Famous writers, fledglings—it's the same all over. And unless you are *religious* about going to the literary readings in your community and attending conferences with other writers, you can't complain. Find ways to build the literary community in your region (but only if you have *extra* hours—this work can't come out of your writing hours).

The skills you have developed as a long-distance writer—staying focused, running your writing life like a small business, avoiding injuries—are the same ones that will serve you as you publicize your book. No one tells you how to do this, but there are good books on it. Check out Lissa Warren's *The Savvy Author's Guide to Book Publicity* and *The First-Book Market: Where and How to Publish Your First Book and Make It a Success* by Jason Shinder.

No one tells you what to do about Free Copy Syndrome. For some reason, many citizens think the author sits on a trove of free copies that she wants to hand out. People miss the idea that we are trying to *sell* books, that this is how we get paid for our work. There aren't really gobs of free copies available. On your own, you may wish to buy fifty or a hundred to give to people. You may wish to direct handout-askers to their local booksellers. Or, like my friend Jack Ridl, a poet, you may, when asked for "a copy of that poem you read," say, "Do you want to trade me? Do you have a painting? I'm up for a trade ..."

No one tells you: People will steal your books at signings and workshops. Nice-looking, middle-aged, suburban people in sensible shoes.

No one tells you people will say things they don't mean

and have no intention of following up on. Many people will say, "We have to get you to do a reading!" Or, "We have to do an interview with you!" Or, "You'd be great on Oprah." Interpret all this as: "Great weather we're having, eh?" And say: "Yes, great!" And expect nothing to happen, ever.

In the end, *you* will always be the person *most* interested in your book. You are the person who gets paid—even if it's only sixty cents or eighty cents—every time you sell a copy. You are in charge of this whole production.

No one tells you: At the end of the day, it's all *you*. This is your thing.

ON YOUR PAGE: *Exercise 35*

How much time are you willing to spend each week promoting your book? What are you willing to do to promote your book, and what kinds of things will you refuse to do? Will you travel anywhere? Will you pay for your own travel? How will you promote your readings and signings? Will you answer all your fan mail? Will someone else? Who will you query about speaking to groups who might be interested in what you say in your book? Take fifteen minutes to brainstorm creative ways you might promote your book—who is going to buy this fabulous tome and why? How will you reach these people? Think about yourself as a reader. What makes you buy a book? How do you hear about books? What would entice you? What would put you off as a reader? Be realistic. Try your ideas out on a writing partner or supportive family members. Can they help? Recheck your daily writing program—where is all this promotion time going to come from? Are you going to be taking time off from daily writing for a few months to do this work? When will you stop this work and return to your next book, or will you be able to juggle both?

Chapter 33

Author! Author!

If you want to write a book, you can write it. If you want to publish a book, there is no reason you can't.

I believe you absolutely should bring your book into the world, that it is right and true and good for each person to contribute one slice to the whole human pie. Putting something of you in book form helps the rest of us piece together the human experience. We need all the books. That's my ideal planet—everyone writes, and we all have time to read. I don't think writing is a luxury or something just for a few talented inspired souls. I want to read your book. I want you to know you can write it. If writing a book is your dream, and you clear out the most common obstacles to that dream—the time thing, the distraction thing, the doubt thing—there's no reason you can't see your book in print. It will take longer than you want it to, make less money than you thought, and be harder than you imagined. But it is so worth it!

In writing books, we are, chapter after chapter, revising *ourselves*—that's how books get written. We learn to do less of what *doesn't* work (overbooking our schedules, staying on as chorale director when we don't have time to write) and to do more of what *does* work (showing up every day to write, preparing the night before, never getting too far away from the book).

Becoming an author was my childhood dream. In this book, I have tried to write down what I did (and didn't do) in order to turn my dream into a bound-paper reality. Probably the most important aspect was learning how to feel comfortable being completely naked, or, if not comfortable, at least used to being exposed. I taught myself how to walk around naked saying to the world, "So, what do you think?" Not an easy thing to do when most everyone else is in clothes. And some people are frowning. But that's being a writer. It's what I always wanted.

Saying "No, I can't come out and play," to my friends Lisa and Jackie and John and Alyssa and Corrine and Jim and Chris and Julie and Pat and Lorna when they want me to come out and play is just as hard as the naked risk. Staying inside when all the fun people are out having barbecues, going on motorcycle rides, traveling to cute nearby towns for lunch—that's not one of the good parts of writing books. I do it only because I will be agitated and unhappy if I get too far away from my book, and it's not worth it. That feeling when the first copy of one of my books arrives in the mail, the little note from my editor, flowers from my Pilates teacher—it makes up for all the missed motorcycle rides, all the late nights reading student work because I wrote in the morning instead of professoring.

It's so completely worth it.

I've noticed if I don't employ my energy into book writing, it turns against me. If I don't use my creative energy productively, every day, toward something bigger than me, toward something harder than I think I'm able to manage, if I don't challenge that creative muscle, it turns on me and eats me up.

The energy doesn't go neutral. It destroys. For many of us, it's not a matter of write/don't write. It's a matter of write/go downhill fast. There's no in between. We're either engaged with this work, or we're experiencing a life crash.

You don't have to publish a book in order to call yourself an author or to "count" as a real writer. The daily habit of attending to this work—mentally focused, spiritually aimed—is worthy in and of itself. The practice of writing works for many of us in the same way that a religious life does. It supports other parts of us, makes us stronger, keeps us growing, while being worthy in and of itself at the same time.

For years, I've worked with talented students who hover just on the edges of a writing life. They *kind of* do it, some of the time. So many writers seem to get stuck in the margins of the writing life; with a tiny bit more confidence, a wee little nudge, they'd be writing daily, with ease, and books would come. Good books. Needed books.

Working through our fear, our lack of confidence, our doubts—all those bad habits of the mind that stall us in the middle of our lives—writing a book gives you a great *shaped project* on which you can hang your growth and development. You can see your progress.

After my first book, I faced my fears about competition and did a triathlon. I learned how to change a tire. I got over my fear of jumper cables. I planted a garden of Japanese vegetables (floundering now). Once I got that book energy unstuck and employed, once I wrote through my fears and just did it, writing three crappy books until I figured out how to do an okay book, I had *more energy. More time.* Weird. But true.

I notice that people who own dogs that are allowed on the furniture generally tend to be happy, well-adjusted, productive members of society. Helpful, good people with depth. Book authors tend to be the same way. Through the training book writing provides, they have gotten out of their own way, so to speak. They have overcome some personal obstacles, some bad habits, they've set their minds to do something, and they've done it. They're good to be around. Accomplishment tends to bring on more accomplishment—the confidence and focus attract good things into your life. Like dogs do. Yes, some dead fish and some vomit and dirt and an awful lot of loose hair. But a lot more good.

You teach yourself to finish a hard thing, and you learn all kinds of better ways of doing things along the way.

More authors!

More authors!

I would love to hear about your book writing. You can reach me at heather@heathersellers.com. Good luck.

Appendix

Books for Book Writers

THERE ARE DOZENS OF TERRIFIC BOOKS ON THE NUTS AND bolts of book writing, and dozens more to inspire writers. To list them and describe their specific contributions would be a book-length endeavor in itself. I encourage you to read widely at your library and then make your purchases. Always choose for quality and then go deep, studying a few books very intensively rather than hopping from one program to the next. However, do be careful. Reading about creative writing is a great way to *feel* as if you are doing something creative. Reading books on writing (especially if you are doing the exercises in them *only in your head*) doesn't count as writing. It can be homework, positioning, or warming up—you still have to write daily *in addition* to reading about writing.

I list here the guides to craft that have been most helpful to me. These are the essential "cookbooks" on my shelf, the ones I turn to again and again. In two cases, I have had to purchase second copies because I wrote so much in the margins that I obscured the text. I read them so frequently, dragging them all over the world—literally—that I wore out the bindings and pages were falling out.

Notice that just like when purchasing music, books that seem great and exciting and fun often become boring after one read, a few listens. My favorite CDs, my most-played videos, are like my writing guides: Maybe they didn't wow me right away, but because they are complex and layered and smart, they yielded a great deal of nuanced wisdom over time. Steer toward books that you have to study just like in school—books that you have to highlight and take notes and review. These types of books are useful enough to earn permanent shelf space in your writing studio, worthy of your dollars and your precious time. (I am interested to hear from you which craft books serve as your Wise Guides.)

I suggest that you keep on your desk one guide to craft, one book on preparing manuscripts for submission to agents/editors, and at least one collection of interviews with writers. Your project will have its own requirements. If you are writing for children, you will want Nancy Lamb's *Writer's Guide to Crafting Stories for Children*. If you're writing a mystery, you will need a guide to the conventions of that genre. My favorite is Robert J. Ray's *The Weekend Novelist Writes a Mystery*. Poets will want *Poets Teaching Poets* by Gregory Orr and Ellen Bryant Voigt, as well as Lewis Turco's *The Book of Forms.*

My list is slanted toward narrative. Every book tells a story. Your study and mastery of basic story structure will inform every book you write, chapter after chapter.

Books on Writing a Book

If you are writing a book in a specific genre—such as erotica, detective, or young adult—you'll want to supplement this list with books devoted to that particular type of book; the Writer's Digest catalog of titles is a good place to begin. However, in general, a book is a book is a book. Books have a shape, an arc, a through-line, and they require similar strategies for organization and development. Below are my top picks for books on "how to write a book." While they are slanted toward the narrative writer—fiction, memoir, creative nonfiction, historical—they're classic manuals on craft, and I think every writer should own them. Plus, you'll get a professional tour of some great literature you may or not be familiar with. Worth their weight in gold are:

Writing for Story: Craft Secrets of Dramatic Nonfiction, by Jon Franklin.

> Franklin, an essayist and two-time Pulitzer Prize winner, teaches how to organize your thinking about your project, which is important if you are applying for grants, residencies, or contacting agents and editors; you must describe your project brilliantly in one sentence, paragraph, and page. Franklin also provides tools for starting a book, getting unstuck, and keeping your project from running away from you. It wasn't until the fourth or fifth time through this book that I really got it. You could apply the techniques here to nearly any book project.

Writing Fiction: A Guide to Narrative Craft, by Janet Burroway. (Any edition.)

> Used in writing workshops—from introductory to advanced graduate—all over the country, this textbook is the bible for any serious student of narrative technique. If you are writing a memoir, creative nonfiction, or a novel in any genre—literary, romance, detective, fantasy—this book presents the essential information you need to write professionally and be taken seriously by

editors. Burroway (one of my teachers) has a theatre background; she is brilliant on dialogue and scene construction, but her "Tower and Net" approach to conflict and structure is required reading. The book has useful appendices—a guide to kinds of fiction and a list of resources—and is chock-full of writing and reading assignments. A terrific final chapter on revision works great for writing groups wishing to focus their critiques and discussion. Look for used copies of earlier editions online or in used bookstores; every edition is great.

The Weekend Novelist, by Robert J. Ray. (Look for first edition, which was printed in 1994.)

Write a book in a year! (For novelists, memoirists, and some creative nonfiction book authors.) Buy this and a copy of Anne Tyler's *The Accidental Tourist.* Read both books straight through (I had to repeat that step several times before I "got" the power and wisdom of the Ray approach). Study *Tourist*. Then, follow Ray's steps exactly. The first novel you write this way will probably be a practice novel, but as you are working, be sure to absolutely commit yourself—write the best, most important-to-you book you can write. It might not get published, but you will know how to write a novel. I emerged with my best novel manuscript to date using his program, and I know how to write a novel now. You can stick with his weekend approach (terrific if you are a busy person), or you can very easily adapt the time structure to fit your own needs.

Books on the Writing Business

For novels, the synopsis (the material you send to prospective agents and editors) is usually written after you have completed and revised the book. For nonfiction books, the proposal (similar to a synopsis) is written first, and then the book. For nonfiction proposals, I suggest Eric Maisel's *The Art of the Book Proposal.* It's clear, easy to use, and very smart. He's published more than twenty books; he knows what he's doing! If you're writing fantasy, romance, detective, or series novels, you should also read *The Career Novelist: A Literary Agent Offers Strategies for Success* by Donald Maass. It's specifically geared toward genre authors. Also check out agents' Web sites for their recommendations.

I use two books by Elizabeth Lyon, who has more than twenty years' experience as an author, editor, writing instructor, and marketing consultant, and is a regular speaker at writing conferences. Her books are *Nonfiction Book Proposals Anybody Can Write* and *The Sell Your Novel Tool Kit*. She takes you through real proposals—successes and failures—line by line, explaining exactly what works and what doesn't, and why. Her comments are immensely instructive, and the books are packed with practical advice. In addition to writing the book proposal (a very specific set of documents you must master in order to break into publishing), she offers detailed instruction on constructing your sample chapter, writing effective synopses, finding an agent, marketing your book, what happens after your first sale, second book queries, and additional must-know resources for book writers. Highly recommended for fiction and nonfiction writers.

Books on Developing Your Mental Game

As you know by now, the main reason books die on the vine isn't because of lack of writing ability. When writers do not attend to the psychological aspects of fear, focus, concentration, and distraction, they are finished by books, instead of the other way around. The three books I have found most helpful over the long term, the ones I turn to again and again when I am stuck, are:

A Writer's Time: Making the Time to Write, by Kenneth Atchity.

> This is an advanced program for serious writers, and I think it is brilliant. Atchity beautifully explains the sophisticated skill set book writers must become comfortable with; he comprehends utterly how the writer must be incredibly wild, free, working from the unconscious *in short, carefully managed, highly structured slots of time.* Both sides of the brain work equally hard when you write a book. You can't be scattered and flighty and writerly, nor can you be too structured and rigid. I adore his system for "dreaming" up a perfectly organized book (and a writing studio, a writing life, and a professional publishing sideline). My writing partner Janis hates this book. If you have a system that works, you don't need a book like this. But I thrive on his note cards-and-files organizational plan; I need a lot of visual stimulation to keep track of where I am in a project. Try it and see.

Writing Alone and With Others, by Pat Schneider.

> Touted on the cover as "The guide that will beat the block, banish fear, and help create lasting

work," this book lives up to its claims. If funds or geography or life situations do not allow you to take advanced college courses in creative writing, this is a great semester-in-paperback opportunity. It's an excellent book to work through with a writing group; it's full of terrific, thoughtful, interesting, and original exercises and techniques you can practice on your own, too. I can't get myself to read this book straight through—I dip in and out. She has the best chapter on voice I have ever read. If you are interested in teaching creative writing, the last section of the book will be your faithful friend. The opening chapters on facing fear and developing habits are just wonderful.

Fearless Creating: A Step-by-Step Guide to Starting and Completing Your Work of Art, by Eric Maisel.

This is the classic workbook for artists, creators, musicians, writers—anyone who is stuck, who is dry, who is further away from their work than they really want to be. Maisel, a psychologist who focuses his practice on artists and creative people (he has some *very* famous clients), has interviewed hundreds of artists; his techniques for working through mental loops and screwy unproductive thinking really work. Buying this book is like having a year of therapy for twenty dollars. You can't do these activities in your head and expect to see results. You have to really do the potato exercise all the way though. My friend Julie Fiedler told me about this book in 1995 when I was deep in a period of depression and not writing; it was the first time the light came on in my writing studio after two years of dark not writing, flailing, attempting, and freaking out that I would never be able to write again. This book, in some small ways, saved my life—my creative self that I can't live without. He has written more than twenty books on all kinds of related topics, but this is the bible, the mothership, the one to begin with. You *must* do the exercises (doing them in your head does not count!). They will change your life, or at least your relationship to your writing life.

Writers at Work: The Paris Review Interviews (series).

Writing is solitary, isolated work. You can get very lonely writing a book. You have to turn down invitations to dinner, roller derbies, the swimming pool, fireworks. You have to sit by yourself in a room, day after day after day. It's really hard to be away from people that much, but there isn't any other way to finish a book—you have to put the time in, butt in chair. The cleverest way to invite people into your studio without losing your momentum is to read interviews with writers. I keep these books on my nightstand—when I have insomnia I'd rather hear a writer talking than the devils in my brain. When I am cranky, feeling sorry for myself, or just needing to get focused in the morning before my writing session, I pick up one of these books and read what other working writers just like me have to say about craft, difficulties, balancing life and art, love, loneliness, jealousy, great reads. If you live in a small town, far from Manhattan, you can create glorious cocktail parties (so cheap!) in your own writing studio by filling it with writer interviews and reading, reading, reading. It's a wonderful way to spend time, to learn about your craft, and to inspire your writing. *The Paris Review Interviews* are seen as the gold standard; I own each collected volume (which includes authors such as Isak Dinesen, Dorothy Parker, Joan Didion, Joyce Carol Oates, Saul Bellow, Edward Albee, and Lillian Hellman). I also subscribe to the magazine, which publishes one or two new interviews in each issue.

Other books of interviews to enjoy are *All I Did Was Ask*, from Terry Gross's program "Fresh Air" on National Public Radio; and *The Believer Book of Writers Talking to Writers*.